A Variety (

(2) Instructions on page 76.   29 cm (11½″) in diameter.

(3) Instructions on page 77. 31 cm (12¼″) in diameters.

(4) Instructions on page 78.   35 cm (13⅞″) in diameter.

(5) Instructions on page **79**.   29 cm (11½″) in diameter.

(6) Instructions on page 80. 29 cm (11½″) in diameter.

(7) Instructions on page 81. 39 cm (15½″) in diameter.

(8) Instructions on page 82.   36 cm (14⅛″) in diameter.

Centerpieces and Doilies

(9) Instructions on page 83.   40 cm (15¾″) in diameter.

(10) Instructions on page 12. 64 cm (25¼″) in diameter.

Materials: Anchor Mercer-Crochet No. 40 White (01) 80 g (2⅔ oz).
Steel crochet hook: Size 0.90 mm (8 steel · U.S.A.)
Finished size: 64 cm (25¼″) in diameter.
Instructions: Make ch 12 to form a loop. **Row 1:** Ch 5 at the beginning and repeat "ch 2 and 1 dtr" 23 times, and work ch 2 and sl st in the beginning ch. **Rows 2–10:** Work around with sc and ch

following the numbers shown in chart. **Rows 11–19:** Work net st with picot. **Rows 20–44:** Work shell at around the outline of pine apple but join with the next shell on row 44. Make 12 repeats of pattern around. **Rows 45–54:** Work net st with picot the same as rows 11 to 19. **Row 55:** Repeat "ch 12, sc in the 4th ch before, ch 9 and sc" 120 times, and end with sl st in top of st of previous row.

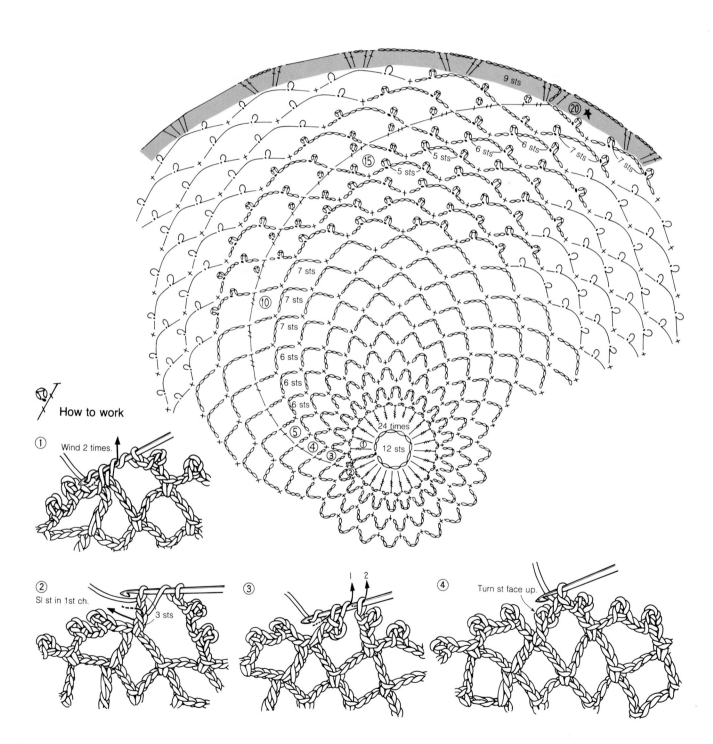

How to work

① Wind 2 times.

② Sl st in 1st ch. 3 sts

③

④ Turn st face up.

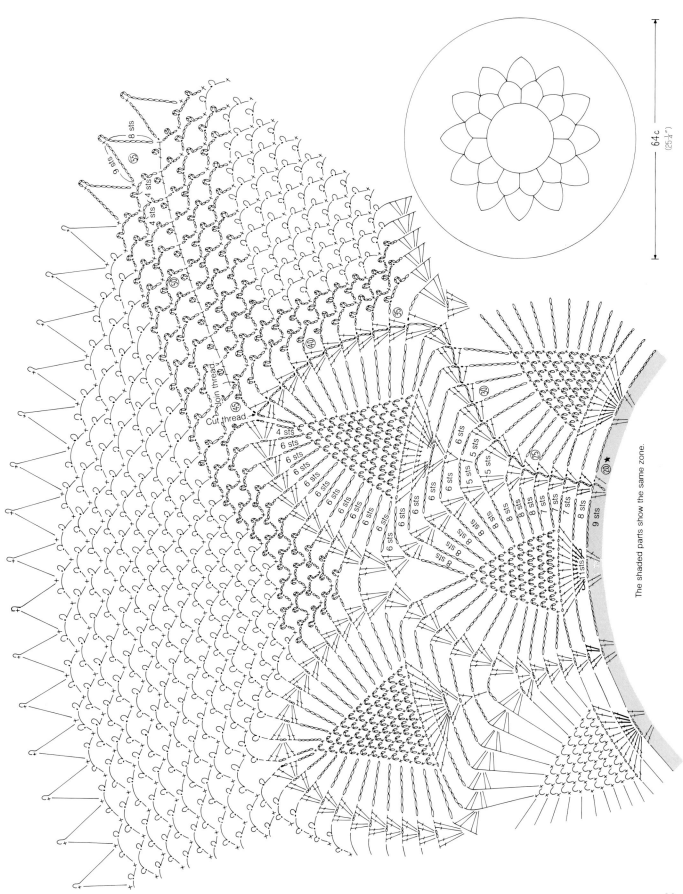

8 sts

9 sts

55

50

4 sts 4 sts

45

40

30

35

Cut thread

Join thread

4 sts

6 sts

6 sts

6 sts

6 sts

6 sts

6 sts

6 sts

6 sts

6 sts

6 sts

8 sts

8 sts

8 sts

5 sts

5 sts

5 sts

8 sts

8 sts

8 sts

8 sts

7 sts

7 sts

8 sts

9 sts

25

20

★

64c
(25$\frac{1}{4}$")

The shaded parts show the same zone.

13

(11) Instructions on page 16. 42 cm (16⅝″) in diameter.

(12) (Bottom) Instructions on page 17. 32 cm (12⅝″) in diameter.
(13) (Top) Instructions on page 88. 31 cm (12¼″) in diameter.

Shown on page 14.

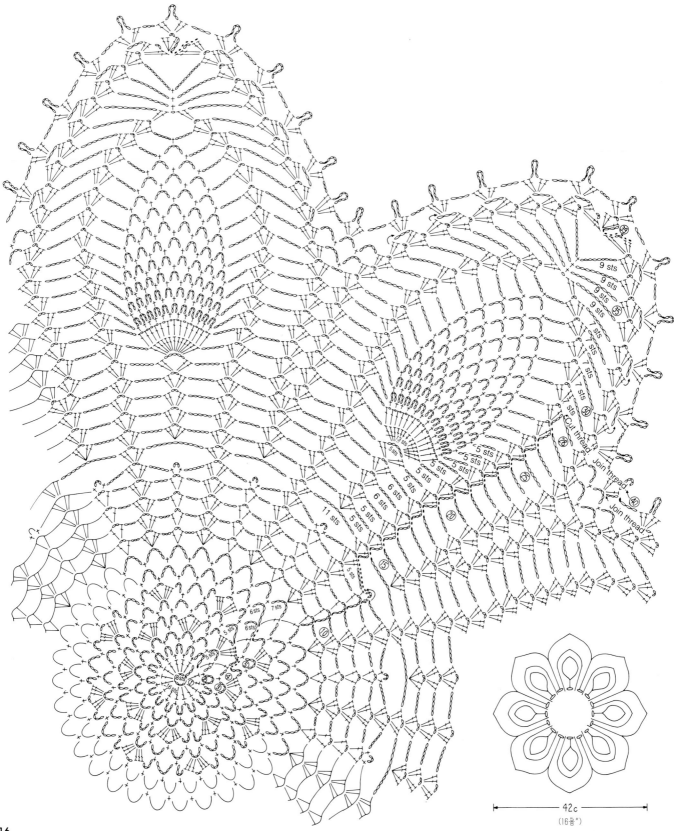

9 sts
9 sts
9 sts
9 sts
7 sts
7 sts
7 sts
Cut thread
Join thread
Join thread

5 sts
5 sts
5 sts
5 sts
6 sts
6 sts
5 sts
5 sts
11 sts
5 sts
5 sts

6 sts 7 sts
5 sts 6 sts
5 sts
8 sts

42c
(16⅝")

Materials: Anchor Mercer-Crochet No. 40 White (01) 17 g (½ oz).
Steel crochet hook: Size 0.90 mm (8 steel · U.S.A.)
Finished size: 32 cm (15⅝") in diameter.
Instructions: Make ch 10 to form a loop. **Row 1:** Ch 4 at the beginning and repeat "ch 1 and 1 tr" 23 times and work ch 1 and sl st in the beginning ch. **Rows 2–9:** Work net st following number of ch shown in chart. **Rows 10–15:** Work net st with picot referring to number of ch in chart; the arrows shown at beginning of row mean to pull picot down toward you and work sl st on back side of picot. **Rows 16–18:** Work around with 12 repeats of pattern, turning the lace to right and wrong side alternately, and work pineapple with shell st along edge.

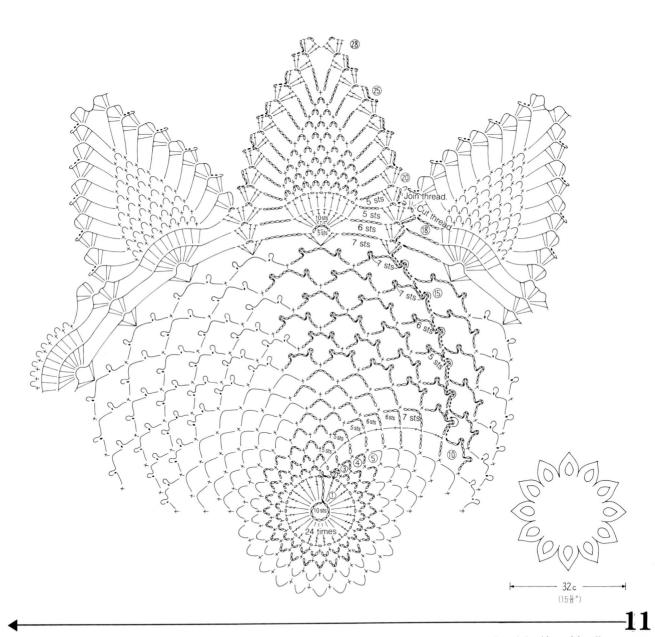

32c
(15⅝")

11

Materials: Anchor Mercer-Crochet No. 40 White (01) 33 g (1¼ oz).
Steel crochet hook: Size 0.90 mm (8 steel · U.S.A.)
Finished size: 42 cm (16⅝") in diameter.
Instructions: Make ch 8 to form loop. **Row 1:** Ch 3 at beginning and work 15 dc. **Rows 2–8:** Work net st with shell st. **Rows 9–19:** Work in radial pattern but work dc on row 9 and dc skipped 1 pattern on row 15, inserting hook into ch of previous row. **Rows 20–28:** Make 8 repeats of pattern with pineapple. **Rows 29–39:** Join thread in each repeat of 8 patterns and work turning every other row. **Row 40:** Join thread and work around to complete.

(14) Instructions on page 20. 37 cm (14⅝″) in diameter.

(15) Instructions on page 21. 38 cm (15″) in diameter.

Materials: Anchor Mercer-Crochet No. 40 White (01) 34 g (1¼ oz).
Steel crochet hook: Size 0.90 mm (8 steel · U.S.A.)
Finished size: 37 cm (14⅝″) in diameter.
Instructions: Make ch 6 to form loop. **Row 1:** Ch 3 at beginning and work 15 dc. **Rows 2–7:** Work pattern radially dividing into 8 parts.

Rows 8–36: Work 8 repeats of pineapple pattern, working the 2nd pine apples between the 1st pineapples. Work shell st as ornament around pineapple. **Row 37:** Work dc on shell st and connect with ch.
Row 38: Work sc and sl st-picot on dc, and sc on ch inserting hook under ch.

25 sts
18 sts
15 sts
12 sts
8 sts
7 sts
6 sts
5 sts

13 sts
5 sts

5 sts

5 sts

6 sts
16 sts

37 c
(14⅝″)

Materials: Anchor Mercer-Crochet No. 40 Beige (01) 31 g (1¼ oz).
Steel crochet hook: Size 0.90 mm (8 steel · U.S.A.)
Finished size: 38 cm (15″) in diameter.
Instructions: Make ch 8 to form loop. **Row 1:** Work 16 sc. **Rows 2–5:** Divide into 8 parts and work around with ch, dc and tr. **Rows 6–15:**

Make small pineapple to row 8 with net st, and work shell st radially.
Rows 16–30: Work pineapple pattern, surrounded by dc and square mesh with sl st-picot in between alternately, to make 8 repeats of pattern. Finish the lace, making frill on the parts worked with square mesh.

Make frill here.

38 c
(15″)

(16) Instructions on page 24.   40 cm (15¾″) in diameter.

(17) Instructions on page 25.   54 cm (21¼″) in diameter.

Materials: Anchor Mercer-Crochet No. 40 White (01) 37 g (1⅓ oz).
Steel crochet hook: Size 0.90 mm (8 steel · U.S.A.)
Finished size: 40 cm (15¾″) in diameter.
Instructions: Make loop around finger at end of thread. **Row 1:** Work 16 sc in loop. **Rows 2–11:** Work square mesh and net at increasing the number of ch. **Rows 12–21:** Work 8 pineapples on base with 11-dc, and shell st surrounding pineapples. **Rows 22–29:** Make the 2nd pineapples between 2 repeats of pattern. **Rows 30–43:** While still working 2nd pineapples, make the 3rd pineapple between the 2nd ones. Work shell st surrounding pineapple as ornament. **Row 44:** Repeat "1 sc and ch 10" 120 times and end with sl st in the top of sc.

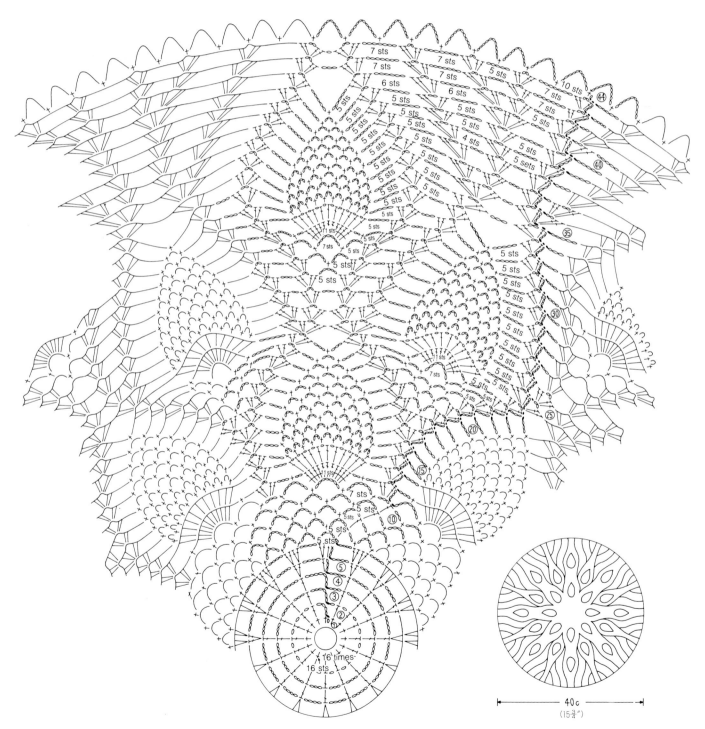

40c
(15¾″)

Materials: Anchor Mercer-Crochet No. 40 White (01) 68 g (2⅓ oz).
Steel crochet hook: Size 0.90 mm (8 steel · U.S.A.)
Finished size: 54 cm (21¼") in diameter.
Instructions: Make ch 6 to form loop. **Row 1:** Ch 3 at the beginning and repeat "ch 1 and 1 dc" at times, then work ch 1 and sl st in beginning ch. **Rows 2–7:** Make 8 repeats of pattern around with dc and ch, and work shell st on row 6 into ch of previous row. **Rows 8–13:** Make small pineapples. **Rows 14–25:** Make the 2nd pineapples. **Rows 26–39:** Make the 3rd pineapples working square mesh between pineapples. **Rows 40–53:** Work around with square mesh. **Row 54:** Work around with 3-tr puff and ch.

54 c
(21¼")

Textured Lace

(18) Instructions on page 28.   74 cm (29¼″) in diameter.

(19) Instructions on page 29.   51 cm (20″) in diameter.

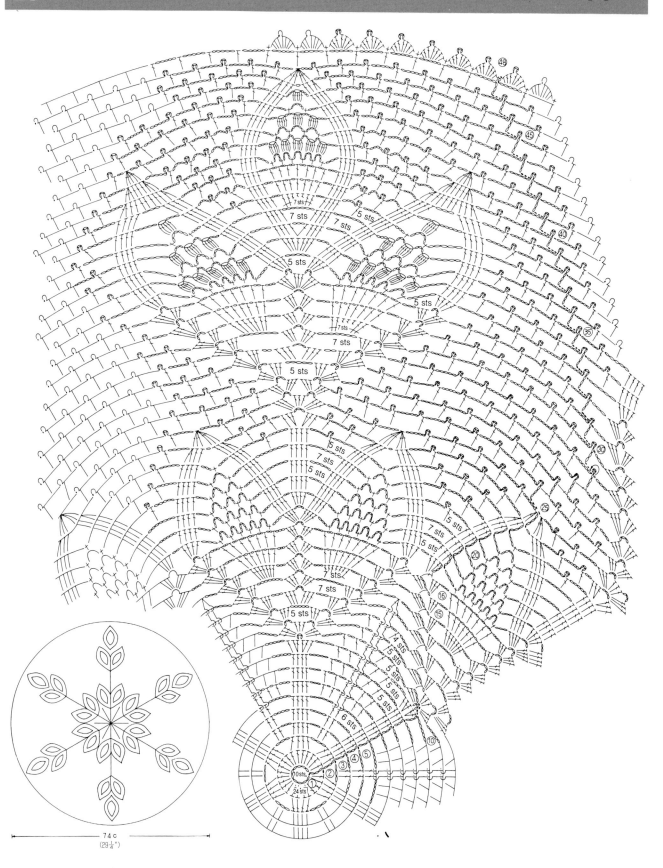

Materials: Anchor Aida No.5 Beige(926) 110g(4 oz)
Steel crochet hook: Size 1.25 mm (4 steel · U.S.A.)
Finished size: 51 cm (20″) in diameter.
Instructions: Make ch 10 to form loop. **Row 1:** Ch 3 at the beginning and work 23 dc. **Rows 2–10:** Work 8 repeats of stem pattern with dc and ch. Work 3-dc cluster at the top of stems. **Rows 11–16:** Work square mesh between the center of stems and 3-dc puff next to them.
Rows 17–32: On row 17, work 5-dc pop on square mesh. Work 3 dc inserting hook under ch of previous row to make pineapple pattern. Work small pineapples between big ones, and square mesh along pineapples. **Row 33:** Work (2 dc and 1 tr) together with sl st-picot.

51c
(20⅛″)

18

Materials: Anchor Aida No.5 White(01) 200g(7 oz)
Steel crochet hook: Size 1.50 mm (2 steel · U.S.A.)
Finished size: 74 cm (29¼″) in diameter.
Instructions: Make ch 10 to form loop. **Row 1:** Ch 3 at the beginning and work 23 dc. **Rows 2–5:** Working around, make 6 repeats of pattern with dc and ch. **Rows 6–14:** Start working shell st on 4 dc from row 9 and raised dc on front side on 2 dc from row 6, and work 2-raised dc cluster on row 14. **Rows 15–24:** Make pineapple pattern with square mesh and net st between shell st and surround with 4-dc, then work 6-dc cluster to connect on row 24. **Rows 25–47:** Work pineapple pattern with 5-dc pop. **Row 48** Work around with 90 repeats of pattern.

(20) Instructions on page 32.   45 cm (18″) in diameter.

(21) Instructions on page 33.   41 cm (16¼″) in diameter.

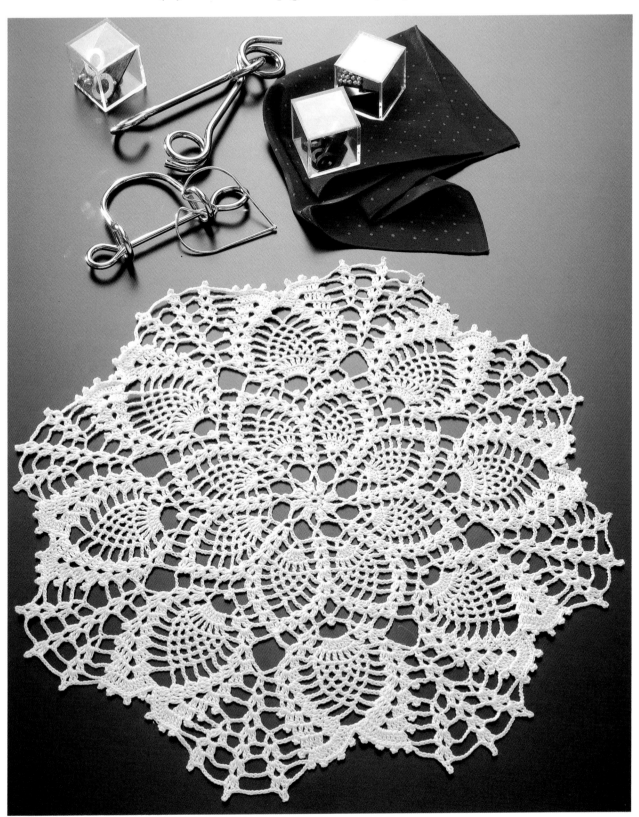

Materials: Anchor Aida No.5 White(01) 63g(2¼ oz)
Steel crochet hook: Size 1.50 mm (2 steel · U.S.A.)
Finished size: 45 cm (18″) in diameter.
Instructions: Make ch 10 to form loop. **Row 1:** Work 16 sc. **Row 2:** Ch 3 at the beginning and repeat "ch 4 and 11 dc" 7 times, then work ch 4 and sl st in beginning ch. **Rows 3–7:** Work around with dc and net

st. **Rows 8–24:** Work dc on row 8 inserting hook into ch. From row 9, start working shell st on dc of previous row and pineapple in between. Work 3-tr cluster on row 23. **Row 25:** Make diamond pattern on pineapple referring to chart below. Complete picot with 3 loops working sl st in sl st at the end of st.

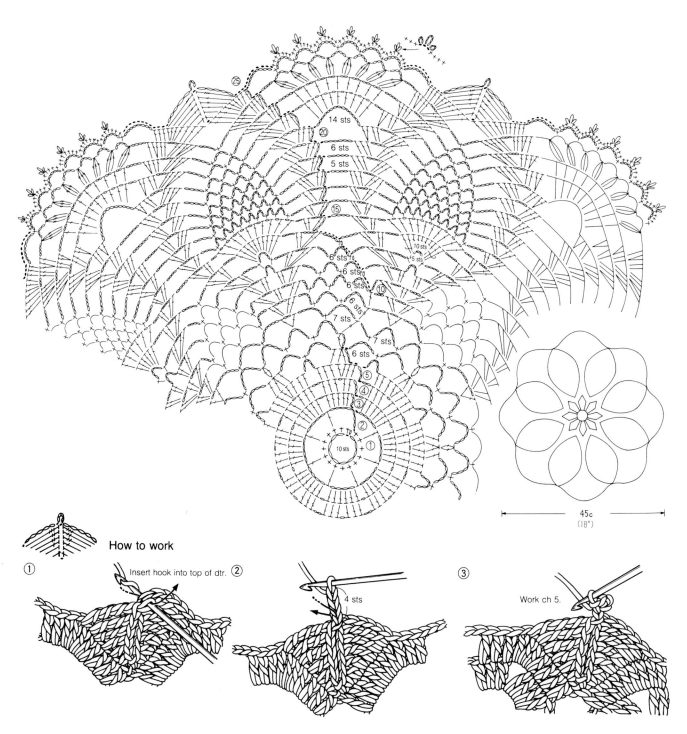

45c
(18″)

How to work

① Insert hook into top of dtr. ②
4 sts

③ Work ch 5.

Materials: Anchor Aida No.5 White(01) 19g(2/3 oz)
Steel crochet hook: Size 1.50 mm (2 steel · U.S.A.)
Finished size: 41 cm (16¼″) in diameter.
Instructions: Make ch 8 to form loop. **Row 1:** Ch 1 at the beginning and repeat "1 sc and ch 4" 8 times. **Row 2:** Repeat around with 3 dc and ch 7. **Row 3:** Work dc in ch. **Rows 4–13:** Work dc in ch on row 4 and make pineapple pattern with dc and net st. Work 2-dc puff around pineapple as ornament. **Rows 14–21:** Work 2nd pineapples between the 1st ones. Work shell st increasing the number of dc, and work picot on edge of shell. **Row 22:** Work around with sl st-picot on sc and sc-picot on dc.

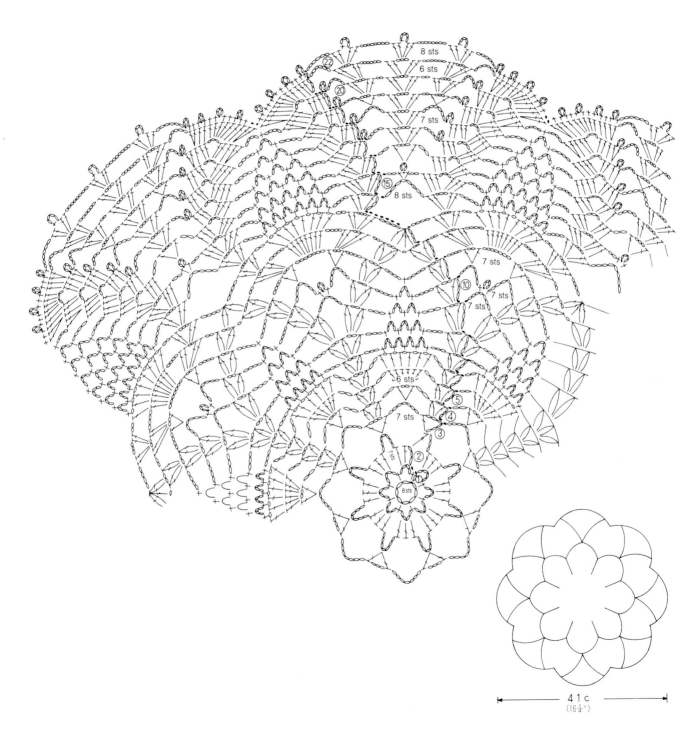

41 c
(16¼″)

Tablecloths,
Cushions,
and Runners

(22) Instructions on page 36. 106 cm (41¾″) in diameter.

Materials: Anchor Mercer-Crochet No. 40 White (01) 210 g (7⅓ oz).

Steel crochet hook: Size 0.90 mm (8 steel · U.S.A.).

Finished size: 106 cm (41¾") in diameter.

Instructions: Make ch 8 to form loop. **Row 1:** Repeat around with 3 dc and ch 3. **Rows 2–4:** Work shell st repeating "3 dc, ch 3 and 3 dc" 6 times. On row 4, work dc in ch of the previous row. **Rows 5–18:** Work 6 repeats of the 1st pineapple surrounded with shell st as ornament. **Rows: 19–36:** Work 24 repeats of the 2nd pineapple. **Rows 37–65:** Work shell st increasing the number of ch between shells. **Rows: 66–78:** Work 48 repeats of the 3rd pineapple pattern. **Row 79** Repeat around with "ch 11 and 1 sc" 240 times and work sl st in the top of hdc of previous row at the end.

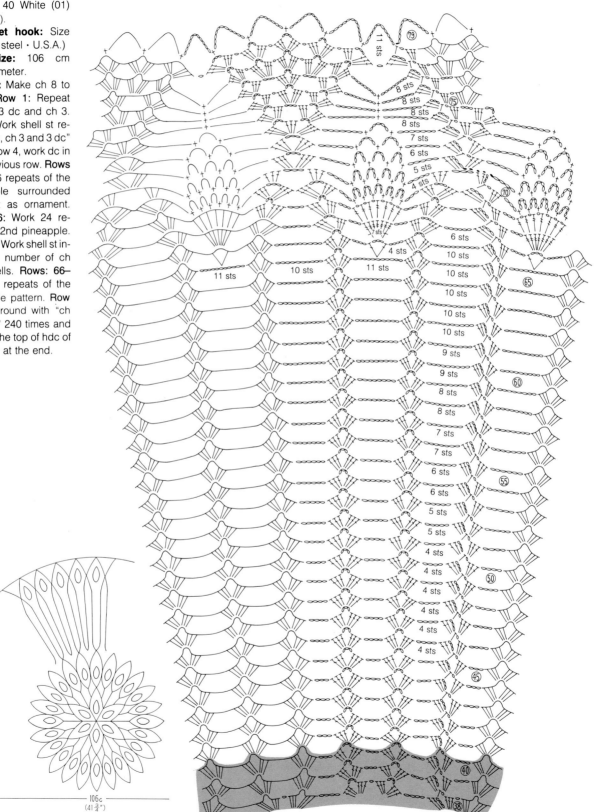

106c
(41¾")

The shaded parts show the same zone.

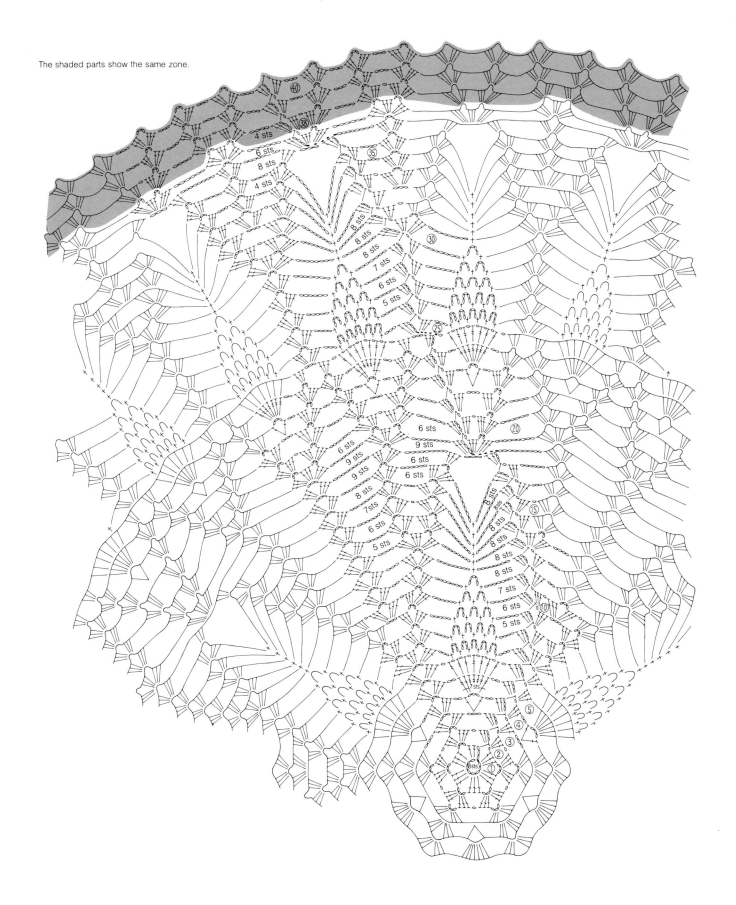

(23) (Top) Instructions on page 84.   42 cm × 42 cm (16⅝″ × 16⅝″).
(24) (Bottom) Instructions on page 40.   42 cm × 42 cm (16⅝″ × 16⅝″).

(25) Instructions on page 86. 46 cm (18⅛″) in diameter.

(26) Instructions on page 40. 25 cm × 71cm (9⅞″ × 28″)

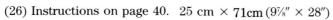

Materials: Anchor Aida No.5 Beige(926) 155g(5½ oz) Stuffing for 40 cm (15¾") square inner case. Dark brown satin 90 cm × 45 cm (35½" × 18") for inner case.
Steel crochet hook: Size 1.50 mm (2 steel · U.S.A.)
Finished size: 42 cm × 42 cm (16⅝" × 16⅝").
Instructions: Front size: Make ch 8 to form loop. **Row 1:** Ch 3 at the beginning and work 23 dc. **Rows 2 and 3:** On row 2, repeat ch 3 and 1 dc, and work dc on row 3. **Rows 4 - 15:** Work square mesh with

pineapple pattern, increasing sts at each corner. **Rows 16–26:** Increasing sts at each corner in same way, work 2 small pineapples on both sides of the 1st one. **Row 27:** Work around with dc. **Back side:** Make ch 300 to form loop. **Rows 1–4:** Work square mesh with ch 2 without increasing or decreasing st. Continue to work rows 5 to 15, increasing sts at each corner. **Cord:** Work with 2 strands. Join front and back together with sc and fix fringe.

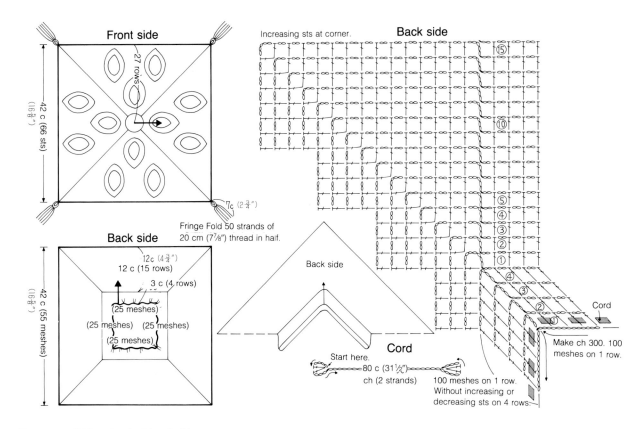

• See page 85 for chart of front side.

Materials: Anchor Mercer-Crochet No. 40 White (01) 60 g (2½ oz).
Steel crochet hook: Size 0.90 mm (8 steel · U.S.A.)
Finished size: 25 cm × 71 cm (9⅞" × 28").
Instructions: Motif: Make ch 10 to form loop. **Row 1:** Ch 3 at the beginning and work 23 dc. **Rows 2–5:** Make the lace around referring to chart. Work sl st-picot. **Rows 6–15:** Change pattern to shape the lace square, working square mesh with picot at corners and pineap-

ple pattern in between. **Rows 16–19:** Make pineapple in same manner but work with dc at each corner. **Rows 20–22:** Work 4-dc puff. Work the 2nd and the 3rd motifs joining at picots to the next motif with sl st on last row. **Edging:** Join thread in corner and work 2 rows repeating "1 sc, sl st-picot with 3-ch and ch 7" and sl st in the beginning sc at the end.

Motif joining

How to work corner

(27) (Top) Instructions on page 44.   26 cm × 41 cm (10¼″ × 16¼″)
(28) (Bottom) Instructions on page 45.   28 cm × 45 cm (11″ × 18″)

(29) Instructions on page 89. 28 cm × 51 cm (11″ × 20″)

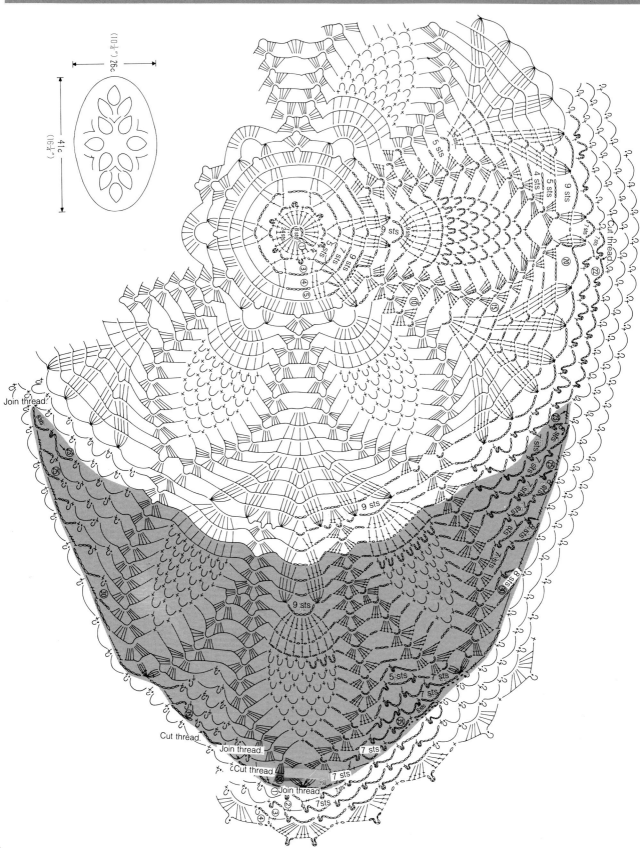

(10¼") 26c

41c
(16¼")

Join thread.

5 sts

4 sts

9 sts

Cut thread.

5 sts

7 sts

9 sts

9 sts

9 sts

8 sts

5 sts

7 sts

Cut thread.
Join thread.
Cut thread.
Join thread.
7 sts
7 sts

Shown on page 42 (Bottom).

Materials: Anchor Mercer-Crochet No. 40 White (01) 31 g (1¼ oz).

Steel crochet hook: Size 0.90 mm (8 steel · U.S.A.)

Finished size: 28 cm × 45 cm (11″ × 18″)

Instructions: Make ch 84 including ch 81 for the center line and beginning ch-3, and work around with 44 repeats of shell st. To work shell sts at corners and on the opposite side insert hook into same ch. **Rows 2–11:** On row 2, work 1st shell in ch, and continue working shell st in every other shell of previous row except both ends. **Rows 12–23:** Make 22 pineapples, surrounding them with shell st. **Row 24:** 2Work shell st with sl st-picot around.

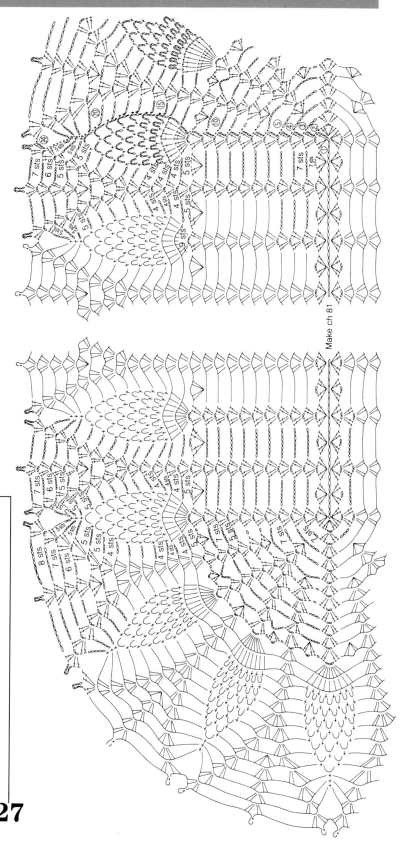

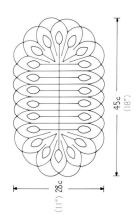

Materials: Anchor Mercer-Crochet No. 40 White (01) 27 g (1 oz).

Steel crochet hook: Size 0.90 mm (8 steel · U.S.A.)

Finished size: 26 cm × 41 cm (10¼″ × 16¼″)

Instructions: Make ch 8 to form loop. **Row 1:** Ch 3 at the beginning and work 23 dc. **Row 2:** Work sc with ch and sl st-picot in between. **Rows 3–7:** Work 6 repeats of pattern with dc. **Rows 8–20:** Make 6 pineapples and work shell st with "4 dc, ch 3 and 4 dc" for decoration. **Rows 21 and 22:** Work net st with picot but work the bases for other pineapples in symmetrical positions to make oval. Cut thread off once. **Row 23–38:** Join thread and work 3 pineapples turning to right and wrong side on every other row. Cut thread off at the end. Join thread and work 4 rows of edging around.

27

(30) Instructions on page 48.   34 cm × 60 cm (13⅜″ × 23⅝″)

(31) Instructions on page 49.   44 cm × 71 cm (17⅜″ × 28″)

Materials: Anchor Aida No.5 Beige(926) 50g(1¾ oz)
Steel crochet hook: Size 1.25 mm (4 steel · U.S.A.)
Finished size: 34 cm × 60 cm (13⅜″ × 23⅝″)
Instructions: Motif: Make ch 6 to form loop. **Row 1:** Work 12 sc. **Rows 2–4:** Dividing into 3 parts, work 3-dc puff at each corner. On row 4, work dc in ch of previous row. **Rows 5–13:** Work puff surrounding pineapple pattern, and work 11 dc on each side to make bases of pineapple on row 5, then cut thread off once. **Rows 14–23:** Join thread to complete pineapple pattern and con-

tinue working puff. At this time, work turning to right and wrong side on every other row and cut thread off. Edging **Rows 1–3:** Join thread and work edging with net st.

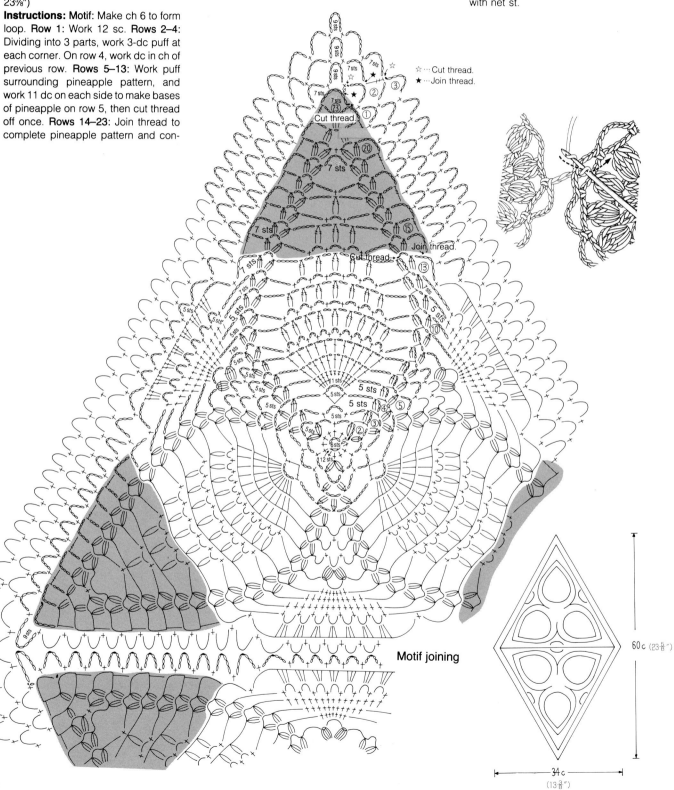

☆ ···Cut thread.
★ ···Join thread.

Motif joining

60 c (23⅜″)

34 c
(13⅜″)

Materials: Anchor Aida No.5 Beige(926) 145g(5 oz)
Steel crochet hook: Size 1.50 mm (2 steel · U.S.A.)
Finished size: 44 cm × 71 cm (17⅜″ × 28″)
Instructions: Make foundation ch 114 (109 sts + 3 sts + 2 sts).
Row 1: Repeat "1 dc and ch 5" and work dc and dtr together at
end. **Rows 2–5:** On row 2, work around on row 1, but work dc on the
foundation ch inserting hook into same positions as row 1. **Rows
6–21:** Work row 6 around with dc, and work pineapple pattern
surrounded by diamond pattern with dc block in square mesh.
Make 12 repeats of pattern in all. **Rows 22–29:** Work 5-dc pop to
form chevron and work around with picot on last row.

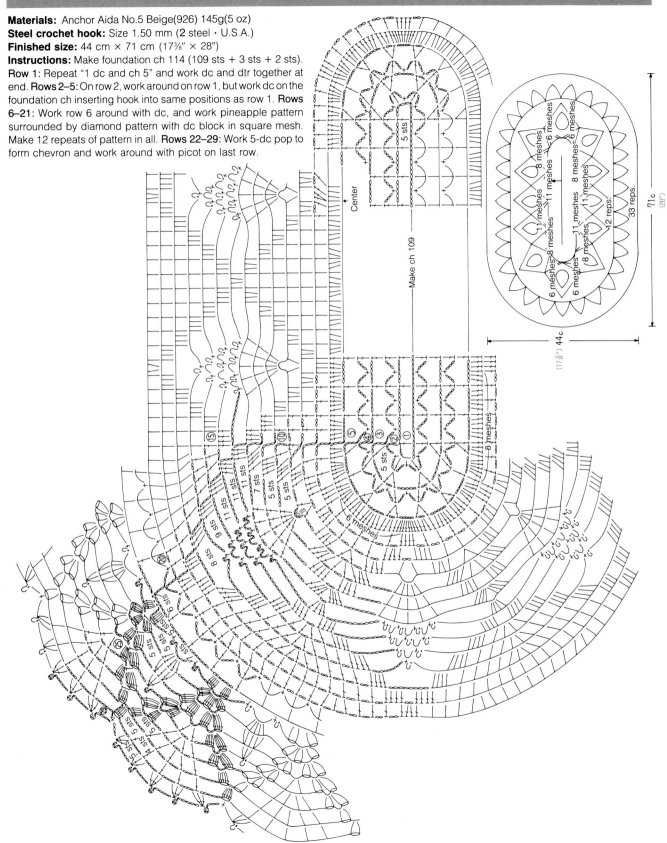

Floral Melody

(32) Instructions on page 52. 25 cm (9⅞″) in diameter.

(33) (Top) Instructions on page 52.   23 cm (9⅛″) in diameter.
(34) (Bottom) Instructions on page 53.   21 cm (8¼″) in diameter.

Materials: Anchor Mercer-Crochet No. 40 White (01) 10 g (⅓ oz).
Steel crochet hook: Size 0.90 mm (8 steel · U.S.A.)
Finished size: 25 cm (9⅞") in diameter.
Instructions: Make ch 8 to form loop. **Row 1:** Work 12 sc. **Row 2:** Work around with 2 dc in each sc of previous row. **Rows 3–8:** Continue working 2 dc radially to make 12 repeats of pattern and work sc and ch in between. **Rows 9–21:** Make pineapple pattern between radial lines of dc, but on row 9 work dc in ch of previous row. **Row 22:** Work around with dc and ch, and end with sl st.

Materials: Anchor Mercer-Crochet No. 40 White (01) 10 g (⅓ oz).
Steel crochet hook: Size 0.90 mm (8 steel · U.S.A.)
Finished size: 23 cm (9⅛") in diameter.
Instructions: Make ch 8 to form loop. **Row 1:** Repeat "1 dc, ch 5 and 1 dc" 5 times, and work 1 dc, ch 5 and sl st in beginning ch. **Rows 2–4:** Divide pattern into 6 parts with 2 dc and make base of pineapple between dc. **Rows 5–13:** Making outline of petals with dc, work pineapples in between. **Rows 14–22:** Work pineapple pattern around with net st.

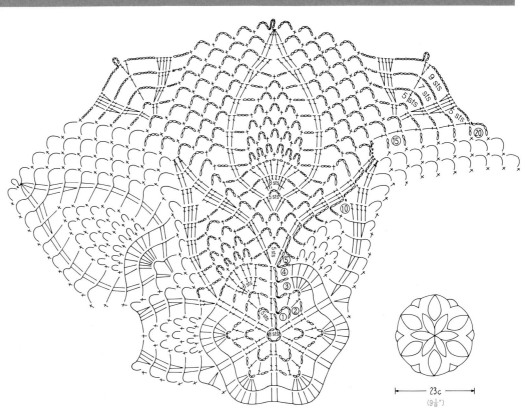

Materials: Anchor Mercer-Crochet
No. 40 White (01) 10 g (⅓ oz).
Steel crochet hook: Size 0.90 mm
(8 steel · U.S.A.)
Finished size: 21 cm (8¼″) in
diameter.
Instructions: Make ch 8 to form
loop. **Row 1:** Ch 3 at beginning and
repeat "ch 2 and 2 dc" 7 times, then
work ch 2, 1 dc and sl st in beginning ch. **Rows 2–6:** Divide pattern
into 8 parts and work shell st increasing number of dc. **Rows 7–17:**
Continue shell st making 8 petals
and work 4-dc cluster at top of petals. Work pineapples inside petals.
Row 19 Repeat around with "1 sc,
ch 4, sl st-picot with 3-ch and ch 3"
40 times.

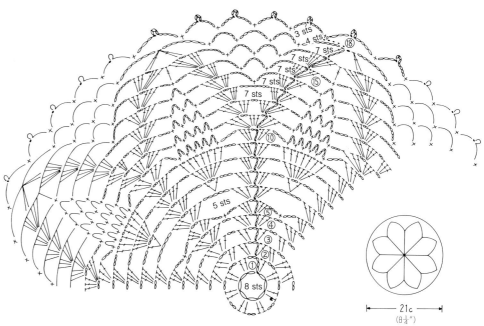

Materials: Anchor Mercer-Crochet
No. 40 White (01) 10 g (⅓ oz).
Steel crochet hook: Size 0.90 mm
(8 steel · U.S.A.)
Finished size: 21 cm (8¼″) in
diameter.
Instructions: Make ch 10 to form
loop. **Row 1:** Work 12 sc. **Row 2:** Ch
3 at beginning and repeat "ch 2 and
1 dc" 11 times, then work ch 2 and sl
st in beginning ch. **Rows 3–12:** On
row 3, repeat around with ch 7 and
3-dc puff and from row 4, making 6
petals with 3-dc puff, work pineapple pattern inside petals. **Rows 13–
19:** Work around with net st increasing number of ch. **Row 20:** Repeat
"ch 5, sl st-picot with 3-ch, ch 5 and
1 sc" 54 times and end off with sl st.

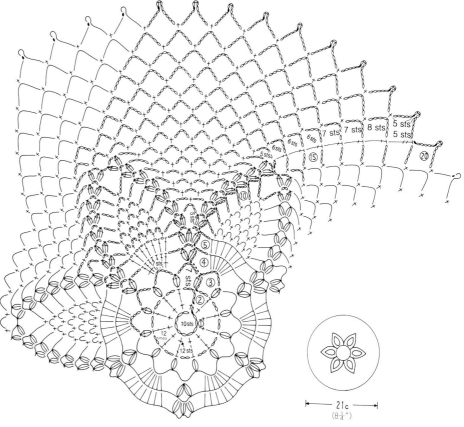

(35) Instructions on page 53.　21 cm (8¼″) in diameter.

(36) (Bottom) Instructions on page 56.   19 cm (7½″) in diameter.
(37) (Top) Instructions on page 56.   20 cm (7⅞″) in diameter.

Materials: Anchor Mercer-Crochet No. 40 White (01) 10 g (⅓ oz).
Steel crochet hook: Size 0.90 mm (8 steel · U.S.A.)
Finished size: 19 cm (7½″) in diameter.
Instructions: Make double loops at end of thread. **Row 1:** Ch 3 at beginning and work dc 23. **Rows 2–6:** Work around with sc on even rows, and repeat ch and dc alternately on odd rows. **Row 7:** Work repeating "shell st, ch and dc." **Rows 8–21:** Divide pattern into 8 parts and work pineapple, surrounding with petals of shell st. Work square mesh between shell st. **Row 22:** Work around with 3 and 4 dc alternately in meshes of previous row. Work 2-dc cluster on top of shell st.

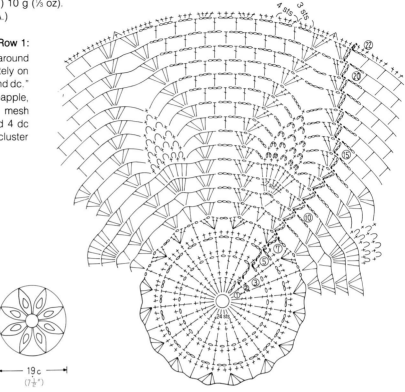

19c
(7½″)

Materials: Anchor Mercer-Crochet No. 40 White (01) 10 g (⅓ oz).
Steel crochet hook: Size 0.90 mm (8 steel · U.S.A.)
Finished size: 20 cm (7⅞″) in diameter.
Instructions: Make ch 16 to form loop. **Rows 1–7:** Work 3-dc puff and net st. **Rows 8–20:** Divide pattern into 6 parts and work surrounding pineapple with shell st, work 6 (3-dc puff) in between, then net st. **Row 21:** Repeat "1 sc and ch 6" 72 times. Work sl st at end.

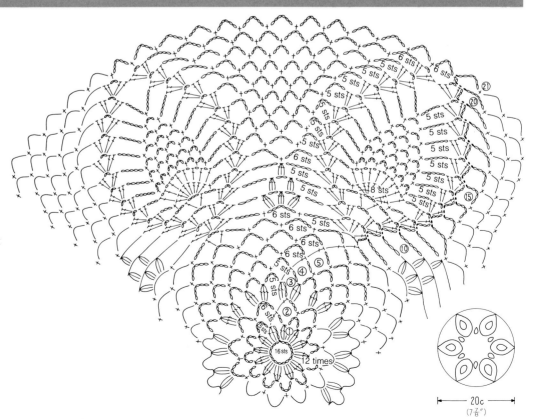

20c
(7⅞″)

Materials: Anchor Mercer-Crochet No. 40 White (01) 10 g (⅓ oz).
Steel crochet hook: Size 0.90 mm (8 steel · U.S.A.)
Finished size: 21 cm (8¼") in diameter.
Instructions: Make ch 10 to form loop. **Row 1:** Work 16 sc. **Rows 2–5:** Divide pattern into 8 parts and work with dc and ch. **Row 6:** To work dc on ch, insert hook into ch. **Rows 7–16:** Work pineapple pattern surrounding with petals of shell st. Work net st on shell st. **Rows 17:** Work net st with picot, dc and 10-tr cluster.

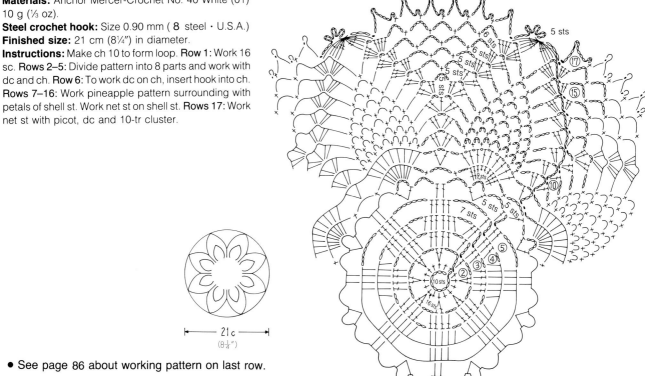

⊢— 21 c —⊣
(8¼")

● See page 86 about working pattern on last row.

Materials: Anchor Mercer-Crochet No. 40 White (01) 10 g (⅓ oz).
Steel crochet hook: Size 0.90 mm (8 steel · U.S.A.)
Finished size: 20 cm (7⅞") in diameter.
Instructions: Make ch 6 to form loop. **Row 1:** Ch 3 at begging and repeat "ch 3 and 1 dc" 5 times, and work ch 3 and sl st in beginning ch. **Row 2:** Work ch and sl st-picot between 3-dc puff. **Row 3:** Work ch on picot and dc on ch. **Rows 4–15:** Work pineapple pattern with 3-dc puff and surround pineapples with shell st with picot as ornament. Work net st and dc between shell st. **Row 16:** Repeat around with "1 sc, ch 3, sl st-picot with 3-ch and 2 dc" 78 times and work sl st in top of sc at the end.

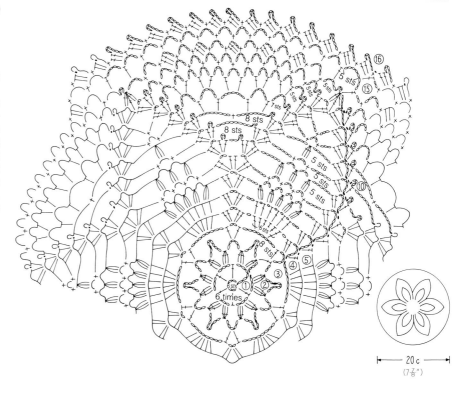

⊢— 20 c —⊣
(7⅞")

(38) (Bottom) Instructions on page 57. 21 cm (8¼″) in diameter.
(39) (Top) Instructions on page 57. 20 cm (7⅞″) in diameter.

More Pineapple Doilies

(40) Instructions on page 60. 38 cm (15") in diameter.

Materials: Anchor Mercer-Crochet No.40 White (01) 30g (1¼ oz)
Steel crochet hook: Size 0.90mm(8 steel. U.S.A.)
Finished size: 38cm(15") in diameter
Instructions: Make ch 10 to form loop.
Row 1: Work 16 sc.
Row 2: Ch 6 at beginning and repeat "ch 3 and 1 dtr" 15 times, then work ch 3 and sl st in beginning ch.
Rows 3-13: Ch 3 at beginning and work shell st radially following

number of ch as in chart.
Row 14: Work petal pattern with dc and ch dividing into 16 parts.
Rows 15-18: Radially continue shell st on petals, working ch and sc in between. On row 15, work 3 sc, inserting hook under ch of previous row.
Rows 19-26: Work pineapple pattern on petals.
Rows 27-30: Work dc and ch radially between pineapple patterns.

38c

Materials: Anchor Mercer-Crochet No.40 White (01) 40 g (1½ oz)
Steel crochet hook: Size 0.90mm(8 steel. U.S.A.)
Finished size: 37cm(14 ⅝") in diameter
Instructions: Make ch 10 to form loop.
Row 1: Repeat "3-dtr cluster and ch 5", and work ch 2 and 1 dc at end of row and continue on to next row.
Rows 2 & 3: Work net st with sc and ch.
Row 4: Work shell st and ch 6 dividing into 12 parts, and work dc

into ch of previous row.
Rows 5-15: Work net st between shell st. From row 7, work sc and picot with 3-ch. On row 15, work shell st on net st to form base of pineapple pattern.
Rows 16-30: Complete pineapple pattern. From row 22, work net st in between.
Row 31: Continue net st around with sl st-picot with 5- ch.

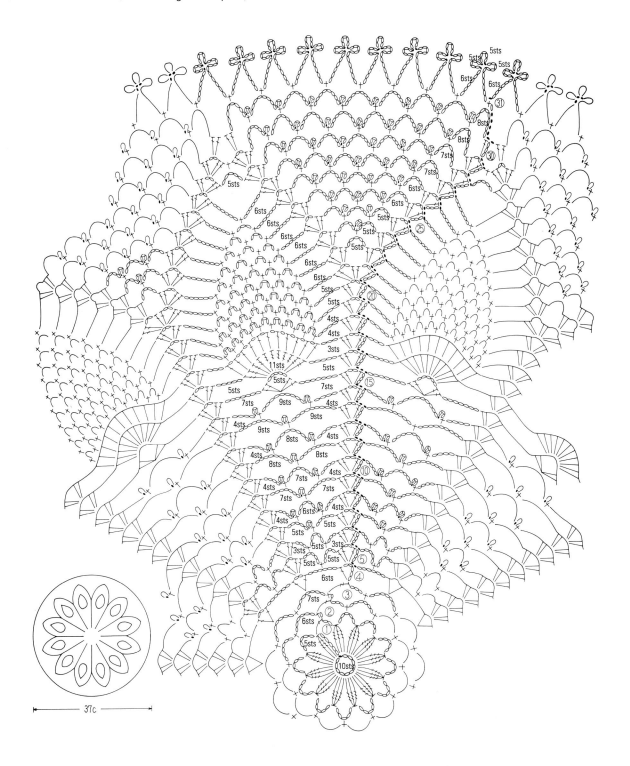

(41) Instructions on page 64. 27 cm (10⅝") in diameter.
(42) Instructions on page 65. 28 cm (11") in diameter.

(43) Instructions on page 61. 37 cm (14⅝") in diameter.

Materials:
Anchor Mercer-Crochet No.40
White (01) 40 g (1¹/₂ oz)
Steel crochet hook:
Size 0.90mm(8 steel. U.S.A.)
Finished size:
27cm(10 ⁵/₈") in diameter
Instructions: Make double
loops at end of thread.
Row 1: Ch 3 at beginning and
work 23 dc.
Row 2: Repeat "3-dc cluster
and ch 5".
Row 3: Work net st around
with ch 7 and 1 sc.
Row 4: Work shell st on net st
inserting hook under ch of
previous row.
Row 5: Make base of
pineapple pattern on every
other shell st, completing 6
bases in total.
Rows 6-18:
Complete pineapple pattern.
On row 16, increase 1 net in
between.
Rows 19-30: Work 24 repeats
of pineapple pattern around.

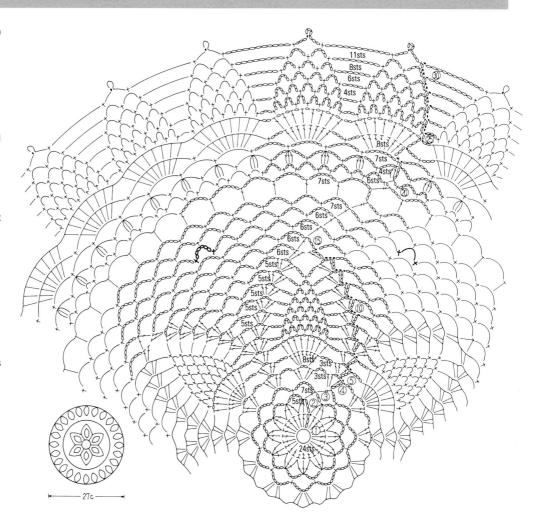

Materials:
Anchor Mercer-Crochet No.40 White (01)
44=15 g(¹/₂ oz), 45=20g(³/₄oz)
Steel crochet hook:
Size 0.90mm(8 steel. U.S.A.)
Finished size: 44=20cm(7⁷/₈") in
diameter, 45=24cm(9¹/₂") in diameter,
Instructions: Both 44 & 45, work the
same up to row 10.

(44): Make double loops at end of
thread.
Row 1: Ch 7 at beginning and work
ch 6 and 1 sc on the 5th ch. Continue
working on row 1 following chart and sl
in beginning ch and complete row.
Rows 2-4: Work radially 16 repeats of
pattern as in chart.

Continued on page 65

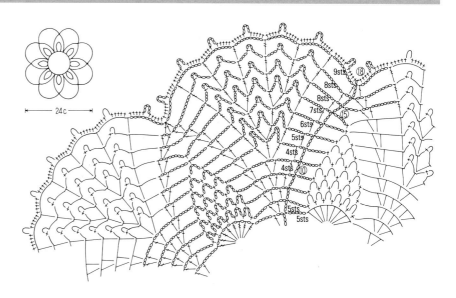

42

Materials:
Anchor Mercer-Crochet No. 40
White (01) 20 g (3/4 oz)
Steel crochet hook:
Size 0.90mm(8 steel. U.S.A.)
Finished size:
28cm(11" in diameter)
Instructions:
Make ch 10 to form loop.
Row 1: Work 16 sc.
Row 2: Repeat "3-dc puff and ch 5"
Row 3: Repeat "4 sc , sl-st picot with 5-ch, 4 sc" inserting hook under ch 5
of previous row.
Row 4: Work 5 dc and picot dividing pattern into 8 parts.
Rows 5-22: Work shell st radially up to row 13 and continue working other rows surrounding pineapple pattern.

44.45

Row 5: Repeat "5 sc, ch 3, 5 sc" and "5 sc, ch 5, 5 sc" inserting hook under ch 9 of previous row.
Row 6: Work base of pineapple pattern on ch 5 of previous row.
Rows 7-17: On row 12, complete pineapple pattern and repeat shell st. around to shape fan.
Row 18: Work 1 sc and ch around.

(45):
From row 11: Work the same as center motif around pineapple patterns.

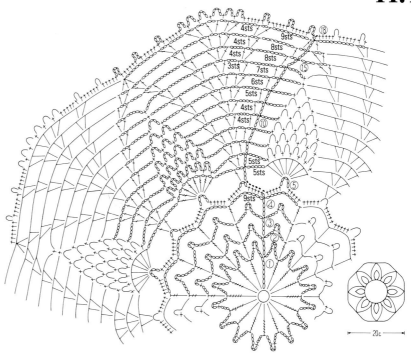

44·45

(44.45) Instructions on page 64. 44=20 cm (7⅞"). 45=24 cm (9½") in diameter.
(46) Instructions on page 68. 31 cm (12¼") in diameter.

46

Materials: Anchor Mercer-Crochet No. 40 White (01) 45 g (1½ oz)
Steel crochet hook: Size 0.90mm(8 steel. U.S.A.)
Finished size: 31cm(12¼") in diameter
Instructions: Make ch 8 to form loop. **Row 1:** Ch 3 at beginning, work 23 dc.
Row 2: Repeat "1 sc and ch 5" 12 times.
Rows 3- 5: On row 3, repeat net st and 5 dc. On row 4, work net st. On row 5, work net st and "3 dc, ch 1 and 3 dc" around.
Rows 6-11: Join new thread and ch 4 at beginning and work 6

repeats of pattern with tr and ch, and sl st in beginning ch.
Rows 12-27: On row 12, work 11 tr to form base of the first pineapple pattern and shell st around. On row 16, make base of the second pineapple pattern in the same way. From row 19, work net st between pineapple patterns.
Rows 28-32: Work net st with ch 7. Rows 29 & 31, work 3 dc, ch 1, 3 dc on every other net st.
Row 33: Work 1 sc, 3 dc, picot and 3 dc around.

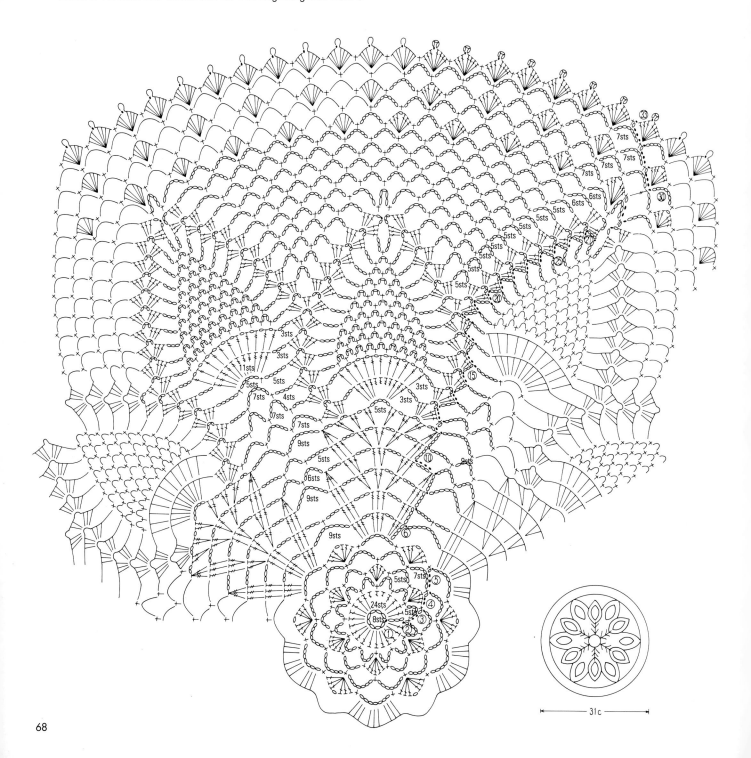

Materials: Anchor Mercer-Crochet No. 40 White (01) 35 g (1¼ oz)

Steel crochet hook: Size 0.90mm(8 steel. U.S.A.)

Finished size: 37cm(14⅝") in diameter

Instructions: Make double loops at end of thread.

Row 1: Ch 3 at beginning and repeat "ch 1 and 1 dc" 11 times and work 1sc and continue on to next row.

Row 2: Repeat "ch 3 and 1 sl st" 12 times.

Row 3: Work net st with 1 sc and ch 5, inserting hook into sl st of previous row.

Row 4: Repeat 4 tr cluster and ch 7 inserting hook under ch of previous row.

Rows 5-9: Work dc radially dividing pattern into 12 parts. From row 7, work shell st with 3 dc cluster in between.

Rows 10-19: Work the first pineapple pattern on dc and work shell st around. On row 19, make base of the second of pineapple pattern.

Rows 20-31: Make fan shape with ch and dc between pineapple patterns.

Row 31: Work sc with picot around.

37c

(47) Instructions on page 69. 37 cm (14⅝") in diameter.

(48) Instructions on page 72. 56 cm (22⅛") in diameter.

Materials: Anchor Mercer-Crochet No.
40 White (01) 65 g (2¹/₃ oz)
Steel crochet hook: Size 0.90mm(8 steel.
U.S.A.)

Finished size: 56cm(22¹/₈") in diameter

Instructions: Make double loops at end
of thread.

Row 1: Ch 1 at beginning and work 8 sc.

Rows 2-6: Work 16 repeats of pattern as
in chart.

Rows 7-11: Work shell st radially as in
chart.

Rows 12-21: Make diamond shape with
dc and sc on shell st. From row 18, work
shell st between diamonds.

Rows 22-32: Work shell st radially
following number of ch in chart up to row
25. From 26, increase shell st from 1 to 3
patterns.

Rows 33-41: Work 48 repeats of shell
pattern radially following number of ch in
chart.

Rows 42-52: Make 24 bases of pineapple
pattern on every other shell.

Complete pineapple pattern and work
shell st in between forming fan shape.

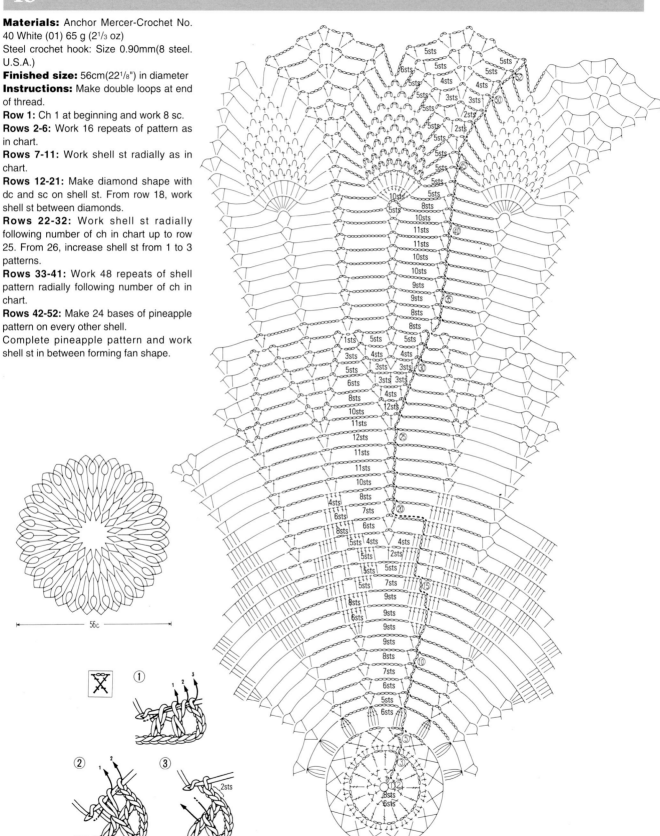

Materials: Anchor Mercer-Crochet No. 40 White (01) 50 g (1³/₄ oz)
Steel crochet hook: Size 0.90mm(8 steel. U.S.A.)
Finished size: 43cm(17") in diameter
Instructions: Make ch 8 to form loop.
Row 1: Ch 4 at beginning, and work 31 tr.
Rows 2-6: Work shell st dividing pattern into 8 parts as in chart.

Row 7: Make 8 bases of pineapple pattern with 9 tr st inserting hook under ch of previous row.
Rows 8-14: Complete pineapple pattern.
Rows 15-26: Work shell st radially following number of ch in chart.
Rows 27-39: On row 27, make 16 bases of the second pineapple, and work shell st between pineapples. ↓

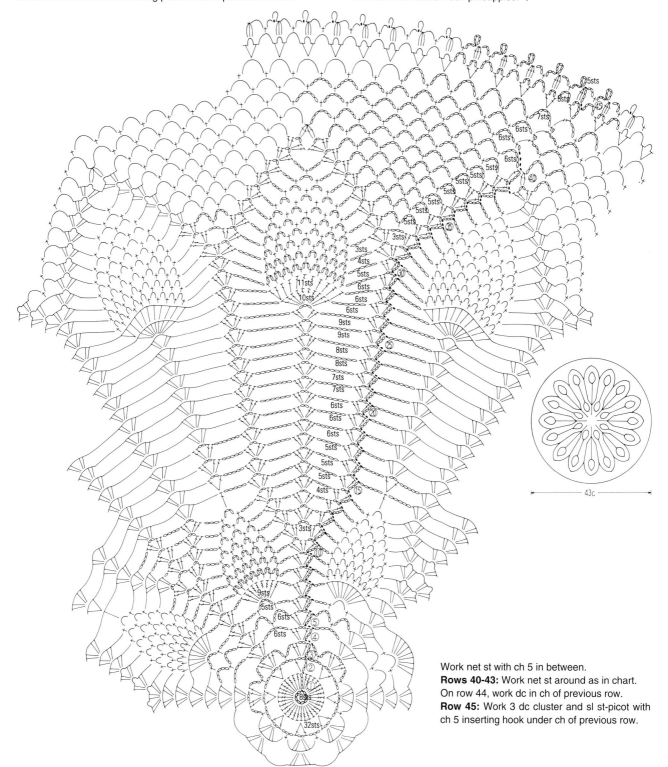

Work net st with ch 5 in between.
Rows 40-43: Work net st around as in chart.
On row 44, work dc in ch of previous row.
Row 45: Work 3 dc cluster and sl st-picot with ch 5 inserting hook under ch of previous row.

(49) Instructions on page 73. 43 cm (17") in diameter.

Materials: Anchor Mercer-Crochet No. 40 White (01) 16 g (½ oz).
Steel crochet hook: Size 0.90 mm (8 steel · U.S.A.)
Finished size: 30 cm (11⅞″) in diameter.
Instructions: Make double loops at end of thread. **Row 1:** Work 16 sc. **Row 2:** Ch 3 at beginning and repeat "ch 3 and 1 dc" 7 times and work ch 3 and sl st in beginning ch. **Rows 3–5 :** Work shell st radially following number of ch. **Rows 6–11:** On row 6, increase 8 repeats of pattern of shell st working in ch of previous row. **Rows 12–22:** Continue working long line of shell st to shape petals and work base with dc, continuing to short line to make pineapples. Make fan shape with dc between petals. **Row 23:** Work shell st with sl st-picot on shell st, and repeat with "1 dc, ch 2 sl st-picot with 3-ch and ch 2" 13 times on fan shape.

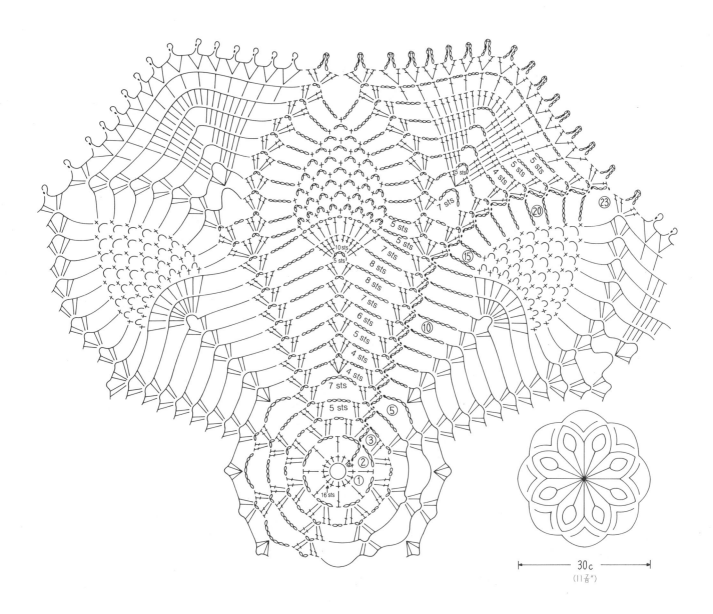

30c
(11⅞″)

Materials: Anchor Mercer-Crochet No. 40 White (01) 23 g (⅔ oz).
Steel crochet hook: Size 0.90 mm (8 steel · U.S.A.)
Finished size: 29 cm (11½") in diameter.
Instructions: Make double loops at end of thread **Row 1:** Work 16 sc. **Row 2:** Ch 3 at beginning and repeat "ch 2 and 1 dc" 15 times, then work ch 2 and sl st in beginning ch. **Row 3:** Work ch 8 between 2-tr cluster and make 16 repeats of pattern. **Rows 4–12:** Make petal with dc and work shell st and ch in between. **Rows 13–25:** Work 8 repeats of pineapple pattern surrounded with shell st. Make fan shape with dc and ch between shell st. **Row 26:** Work "2 dc, sl st-picot with 5-ch and 2 dc" on shell st, and repeat "3 dc, sl st-picot with 5-ch and 3 dc" 7 times on fan shape. Make 8 repeats of pattern in all. Finish the beginning and end of thread.

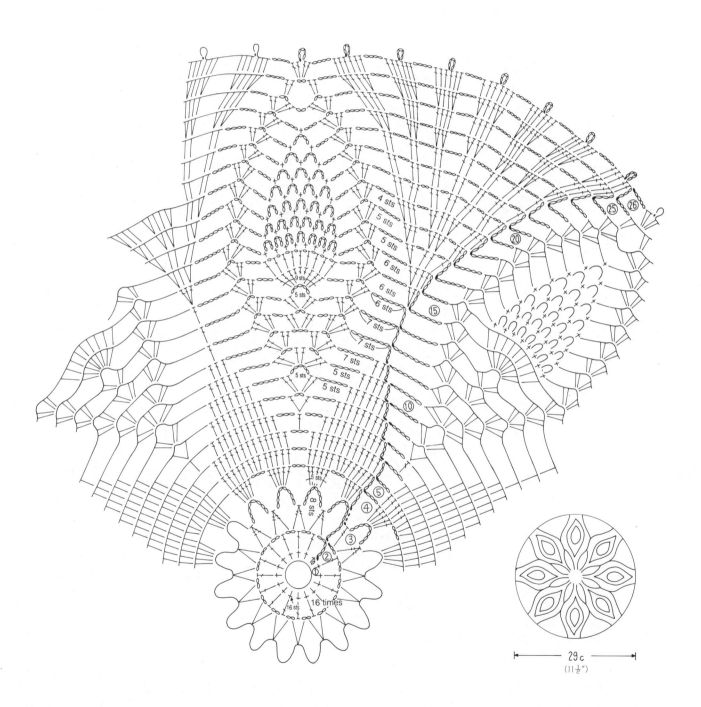

29 c
(11½")

Materials: Anchor Mercer-Crochet No. 40 White (01) 21 g (¾ oz).
Steel crochet hook: Size 0.90 mm (8 steel · U.S.A.)
Finished size: 31 cm (12¼″) in diameter.
Instructions: Make ch 6 to form loop. **Row 1:** Ch 3 at beginning and repeat "ch 1 and 1 dc" 11 times. Work ch 1 and sl st in beginning ch.
Rows 2–13: Divide pattern into 12 parts, and work shell st, dc and ch

in radial pattern, adjusting with ch between each st. **Rows 14–22:** Continue working shell st to shape petals, and make base with 7 dc for pineapple inside petal. **Rows 23–28:** Work around net st with "1 sc and ch 5." **Row 29** Work "ch 3, 7 dc, ch 3 and 1 sc" in every 2 loops of previous row to make 60 repeats.

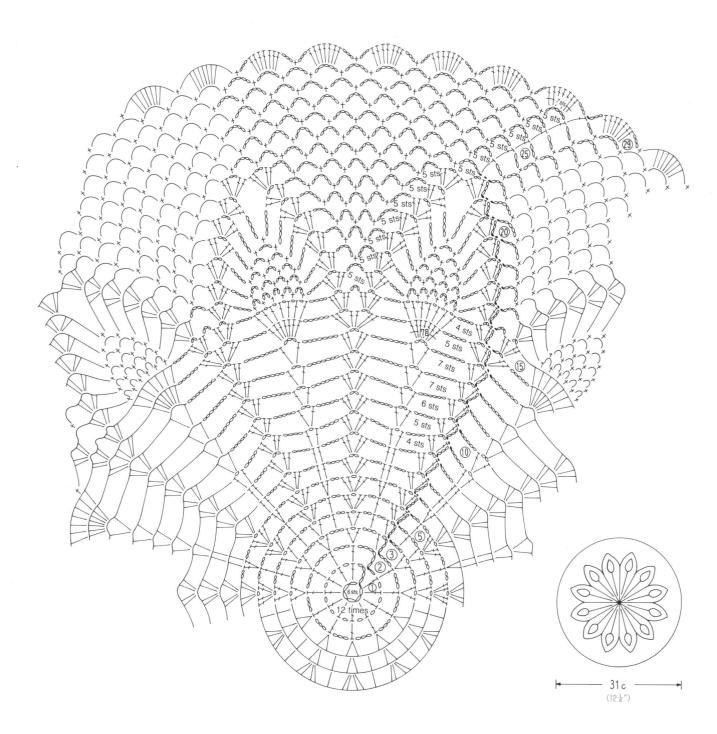

31c
(12¼″)

Materials: Anchor Mercer-Crochet No. 40 White (01) 20 g (¾ oz).
Steel crochet hook: Size 0.90 mm (8 steel · U.S.A.)
Finished size: 35 cm (13⅞″) in diameter.
Instructions: Make ch 6 to form loop. **Rows 1 and 2:** Ch 3 at beginning and work square mesh increasing number of ch. **Row 3:** Work with sc and ch. **Rows 4–14:** Divide pattern into 8 parts, and work pineapple pattern between radial lines with 4 tr. Make base with 7 tr. **Rows 15–27:** Continue working radial line with tr and make new radial line with tr on 1st pineapples. Work 16 repeats of 2nd pineapple pattern between tr.

35c
(13⅞″)

5

Shown on page 6.

Materials: Anchor Mercer-Crochet No. 40 White (01) 23 g (⅔ oz).
Steel crochet hook: Size 0.90 mm (8 steel · U.S.A.)
Finished size: 29 cm (11½") in diameter.
Instructions: Make ch 6 to form loop. **Row 1:** Ch 3 at beginning and work 15 dc. **Row 2:** Work ch 1 between dc. **Rows 3–10:** Divide pattern into 8 parts and work shell st radially. Work sc and ch in between to make pattern. **Rows 11–24:** From row 8 work shell st, parting in middle to make petals. Work pineapples inside petals after making base with 11 tr. Work increasing dc between petals, and on row 20 work 7 tr for base of 2nd pineapple pattern. **Rows 25–28:** Work small pineapples surrounded with dc. **Row 29:** Repeat "1 sc, ch 3 and 3 dc" 120 times but work 3 dc into sc.

79

Materials: Anchor Mercer-Crochet No. 40 White (01) 20 g (¾ oz).
Steel crochet hook: Size 0.90 mm (8 steel · U.S.A.)
Finished size: 29 cm (11½") in diameter.
Instructions: Make ch 10 to form loop. **Row 1:** Ch 3 at beginning and work 23 dc. **Rows 2–15:** Divide pattern into 4 parts and make petals with shell st. Work pineapple pattern inside petals. **Rows 16–24:** Work triangular pattern with dc on pineapples and make 2 petals along pineapples between triangles. **Row 25 and 26:** Work around sts with picots.

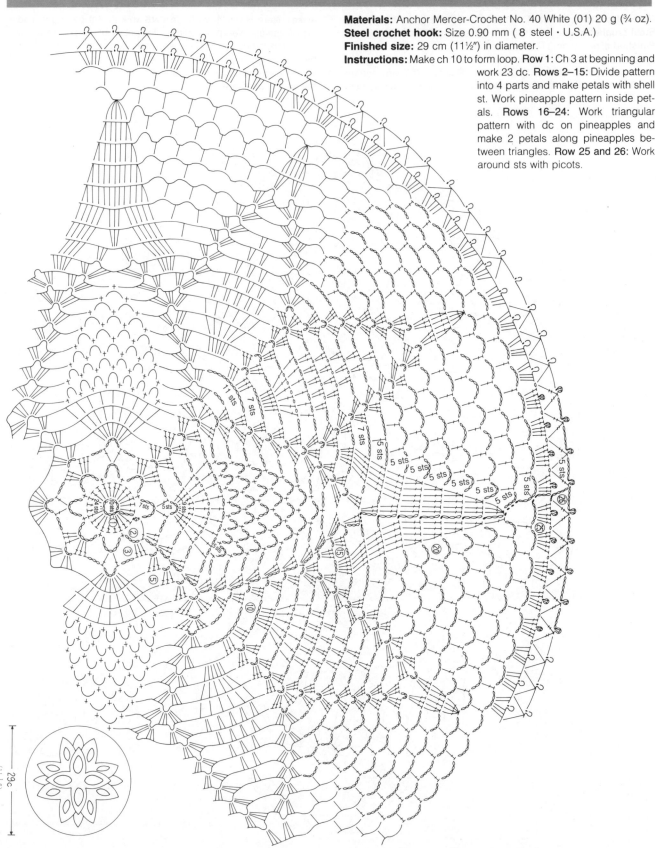

29c
(11½")

80

Materials: Anchor Mercer-Crochet No. 40 White (01) 32 g (1¼ oz).
Steel crochet hook: Size 0.90 mm (8 steel · U.S.A.)
Finished size: 39 cm (15½″) in diameter.
Instructions: Make ch 5 to form loop. **Row 1:** Ch 3 at beginning and repeat "ch 1 and 2 dc" 7 times. Work ch 1, 1 dc and sl st at beginning ch. **Rows 2–12:** Divide pattern into 8 parts and make petals with shell st. On row 10, work 10 dc for base of pineapple outside petals. **Rows 13– 23:** Make 2nd petals between 1st ones with shell st and work pineapples inside. **Rows 24–31:** Work around with net st increasing number of ch. **Row 32:** Repeat "2 tr, ch 3, sl st-picot with 3-ch, ch 3, 2 tr and 1 sc" 64 times and end with sl st in top of tr of previous row.

Materials: Anchor Mercer-Crochet No. 40 White (01) 29 g (1 oz).
Steel crochet hook: Size 0.90 mm (8 steel · U.S.A.)
Finished size: 36 cm (14⅛″) in diameter.
Instructions: Make ch 8 to form loop. **Row 1:** Ch 3 at beginning and repeat "ch 1 and 1 dc" 15 times. Work ch 1 and sl st in beginning. **Rows 2–5:** Work dc on row 2 and 5, and net st on row 3 and 4. **Rows 6–10:** Work around net st with 5-ch but shell st on every other loop on row 10. **Rows 11–20:** Work shell st on shell st at every repeat of pattern to shape petals, and make base with 8 dc inside to work pineapple pattern. On row 17, make base of next pineapples with 10 dc between petals. **Rows 21–28:** Make petals continuing shell st and work pineapple pattern inside. **Rows 29–37:** Work last row around with shell st with picot.

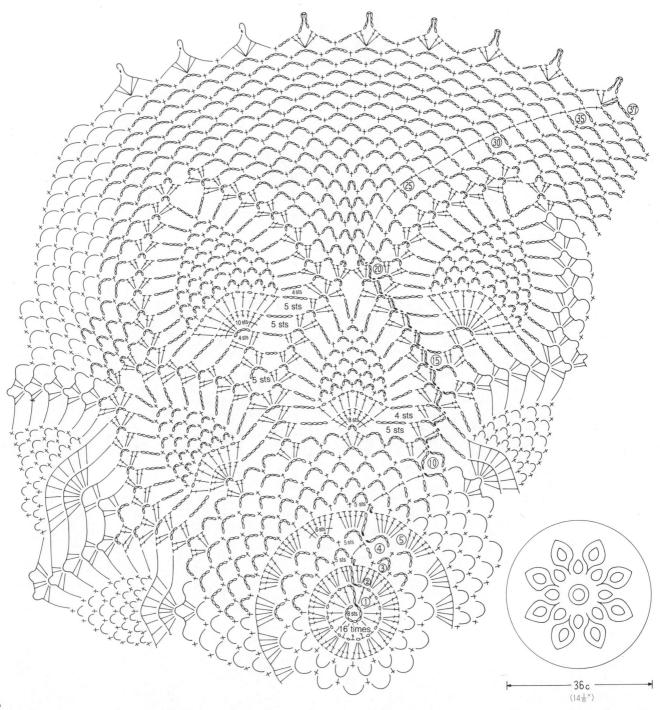

Materials: Anchor Mercer-Crochet No. 40 White (01) 44 g (1½ oz).
Steel crochet hook: Size 0.90 mm (8 steel · U.S.A.)
Finished size: 40 cm (15¾") in diameter.
Instructions: Make ch 8 to form loop. **Row 1:** Ch 4 at beginning and work 31 tr and sl st. **Row 2:** Ch 3 at beginning and work 1 dc and "ch 2 and 2 dc" 15 times. Work ch 2 and sl st at beginning ch. **Rows 3–23:** Work 8 repeats of petal with 3-dc puff. Make pineapple pattern inside and work net st with 5-ch between petals. **Rows 24–40:** Work around with net st increasing number of ch but work shell st on every 4 loops. **Row 41:** Work tr with sl st-picot and ch 10 alternately.

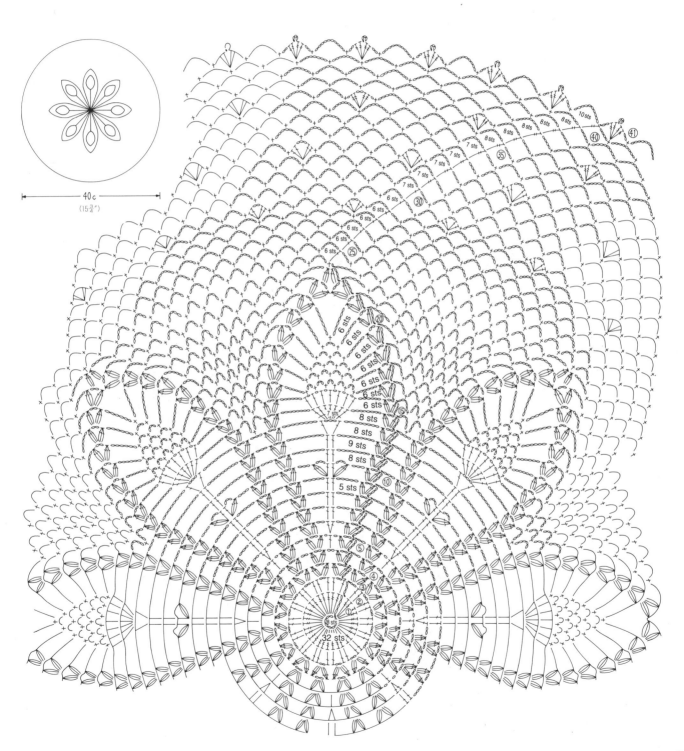

40 c
(15¾")

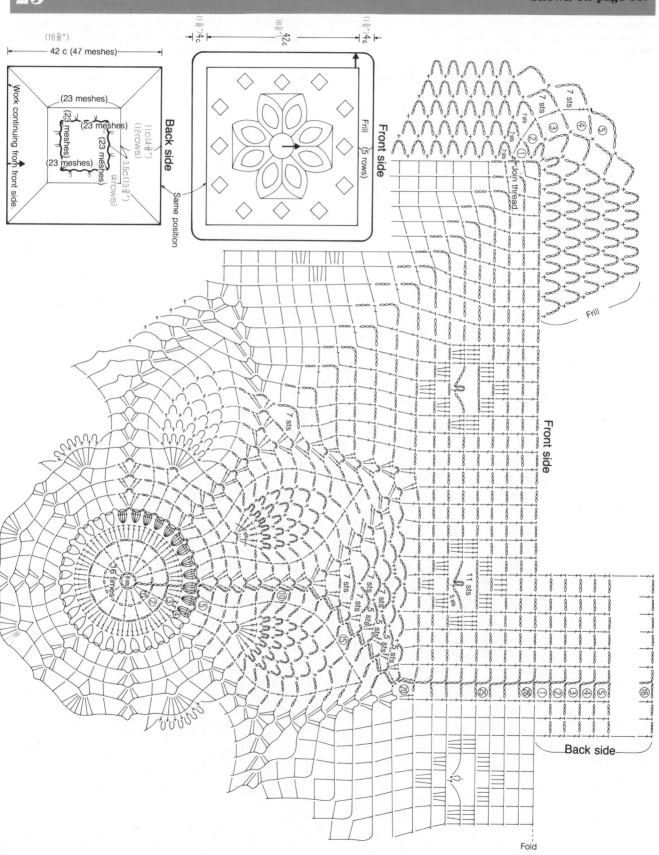

Materials: Anchor Aida No.5 Beige(926) 145g (5 oz)
Stuffing for 40 cm (15¾") square inner cushion. Gray satin
90 cm × 45 cm (35½" × 17¾") for inner cushion.
Steel crochet hook: Size 1.50 mm (2 steel · U.S.A.)
Finished size: 42 cm × 42 cm (16⅝" × 16⅝").
Instructions: Front side: Make ch 8 to form loop. **Rows 1
and 2:** Work square mesh following number of ch. **Row 3:**
Work around with dc. **Row 4:** Work 5-dc pop in every
other dc of previous row. **Rows 5–19:** Make petal with shell
st and work pineapples inside petals. Divide pattern into 4
parts and increase sts of square mesh at corners and work
net st on sides. **Rows 20–28:** Work square mesh increasing
sts at each corner. **Back side:** Continue and work decreasing sts at each corner. Make cord with 2 strands and work
frill on the folding line between back and front side.

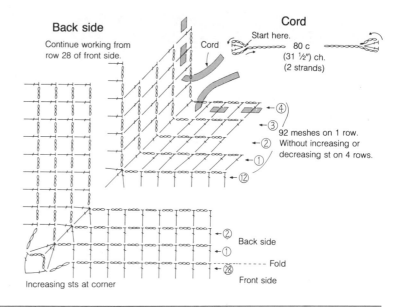

Back side

Continue working from
row 28 of front side.

Cord

Start here.

80 c
(31 ½") ch.
(2 strands)

④
③
② 92 meshes on 1 row.
① Without increasing or
⑫ decreasing st on 4 rows.

② Back side
①
⑱ - - - Fold
Front side

Increasing sts at corner

● The work No. 24　Continue from page 40.

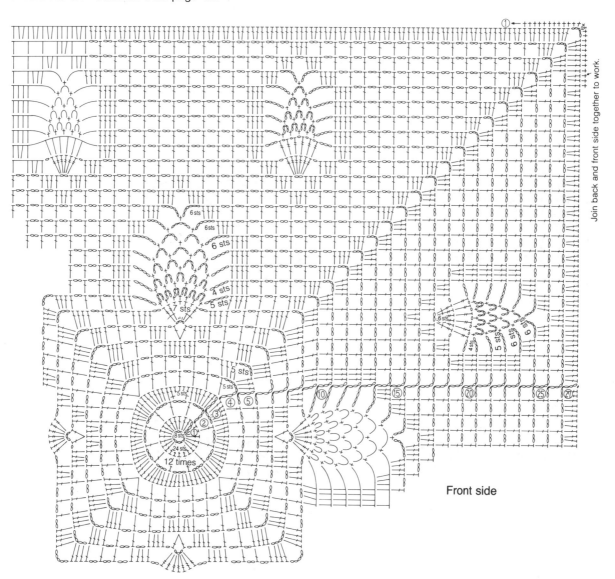

Front side

Materials: Anchor Mercer-Crochet No. 40 White (01) 120 g (4¼ oz). Stuffing for 45 cm (17¾") round inner cushion. Pink satin 47 cm × 92 cm (18½" × 36¼") for inner cushion.
Steel crochet hook: Size 0.90 mm (8 steel · U.S.A.)
Finished size: 46 cm (18⅛") in diameter.
Instructions: Make ch 8 to form loop. **Row 1:** Ch 3 at beginning, and work 23 dc and sl st in beginning ch. **Row 2:** Ch 3 at beginning, and work ch 1 and 1 dc. Work "1 dc, ch 1 and 1 dc" in every other dc of previous row and make 11 repeats of pattern. **Rows 3–9:** Work shell st radially and connect shell st with dc and ch. **Rows 10–25:** Continue working shell st to shape petals and work pineapples inside. On row 13 (row 22), work dc in ch 7 (ch 5) of previous row inserting hook into ch. Make base of next pineapple with 10 dc on row 23. **Rows 26–35:** Continue working shell st to make 2nd petals. Work pineapples inside and net st between petals. **Rows 36–40:** Work around with net st with 6-ch. Work front and back sides in same way. Do not cut thread at the end of 2nd piece. Join 2 pieces together with repeating "ch 3, sl st in net st on another piece, ch 3 and 1 sc" but after joining two thirds, put inner pillow in and complete joining.

● The work No. 38 Continue from page 57. ——————————————————

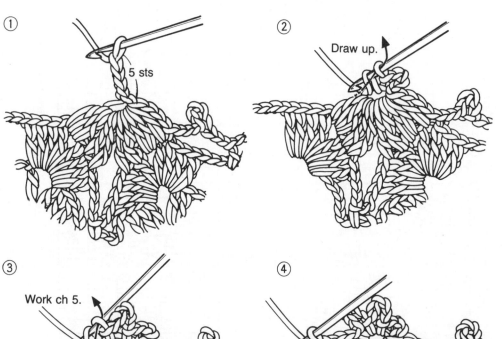

① After working 10 sts of dc and tr together, work ch 5.
② Work sl st in back loop of 1st ch.
③ Work ch 5, sl st in same st and ch 5 again.
④ Work sl st in same st again, ch 3 and sl st in root of last dc.

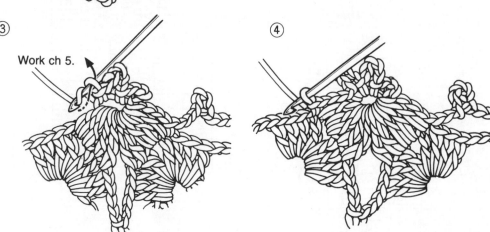

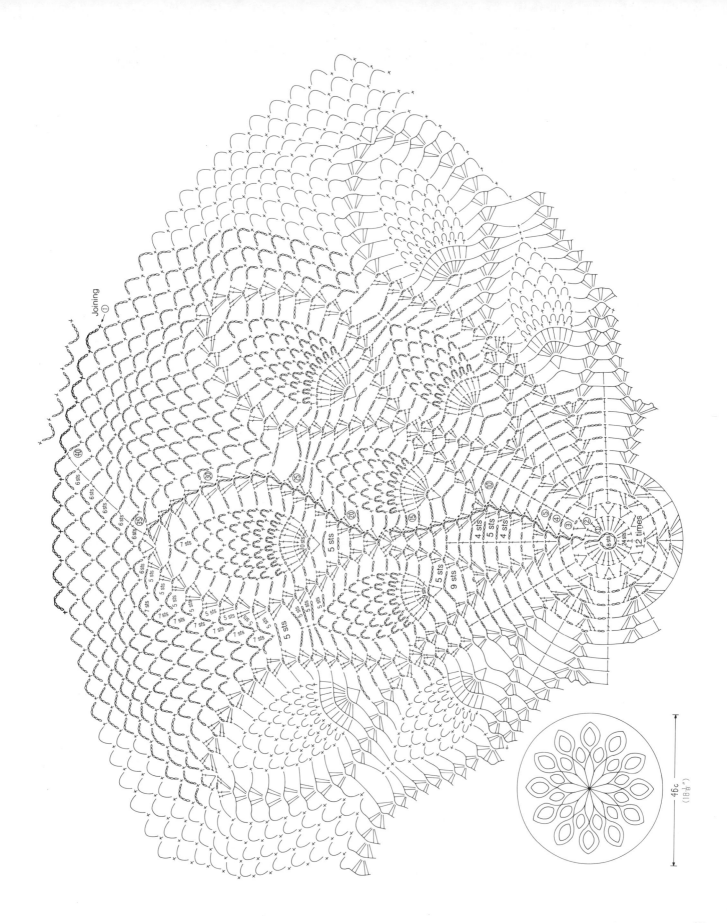

Joining ①

④⓪

6 sts
6 sts
6 sts
6 sts
⑤⑤
6 sts
6 sts

③⓪

②⑤

7 sts
7 sts
7 sts
7 sts
5 sts
5 sts
5 sts
5 sts
5 sts
5 sts

②⓪

10 sts
5 sts

5 sts

①⑤

9 sts

5 sts
5 sts
9 sts

⑩

4 sts
5 sts
4 sts

⑤
④
③
②
①

8 sts
24 sts
12 times

46c
(18⅛")

Materials: Anchor Mercer-Crochet No. 40 White (01) 24 g (⅔ oz).
Steel crochet hook: Size 0.90 mm (8 steel · U.S.A.)
Finished size: 31 cm (12¼″) in diameter.
Instructions: Make ch 6 to form loop. **Row 1:** Ch 1 at beginning and work 8 sc in a loop. **Row 2:** Ch 1 at beginning and repeat "1 sc and ch 5" 7 times. Work 1 sc, ch 2 and 1 dc at end of row. **Rows 3–7:** Work with dc and net st. Work net st changing number of ch on every row. **Row 8:** Work around with 7 sc in 1 loop of previous row. **Rows 9–18:**

Divide pattern into 8 parts and make plant with dc and 5-dc pop. Work 1 dc and ch 5 alternately between plants. **Rows 19 and 20:** Work net st with 5-ch. **Rows 21–23:** Make base of pineapple with 7 dc and work 2 pineapples in 1 repeat of pattern. Work net st in between and cut thread at end. **Row 24–30:** Join thread in every 16 pineapples to complete. Join thread at center of shell st and work on front and back side alternately.

31c
(12¼″)

88

Shown on page 43.

Materials: Anchor Mercer-Crochet No. 40 White (01) 39 g (1⅓ oz).
Steel crochet hook Size: 0.90 mm (8 steel · U.S.A.)
Finished size: 28 cm × 51 cm (11″ × 20″)
Instructions: Make foundation ch 111 at center of oval. **Row 1:** Ch3 at beginning, and work dc, sc and ch. Make 6 repeats of pattern on each side along straight line and 1 repeat on each corner. **Rows 2–4:**

Work around with dc and net st. **Rows 5–18:** Working with 3-dc puff, make 7 petals each along straight line and 3 petals on each corner. Work pineapples on the base with 9 tr inside petals. **Rows 19–23:** Work around net st with 5-ch at row 19 and with 6-ch until row 23. **Row 24:** Work 3 (3-dc puff) in every other loop of previous row. **Row 25:** work ch 5 and ch 7 alternately.

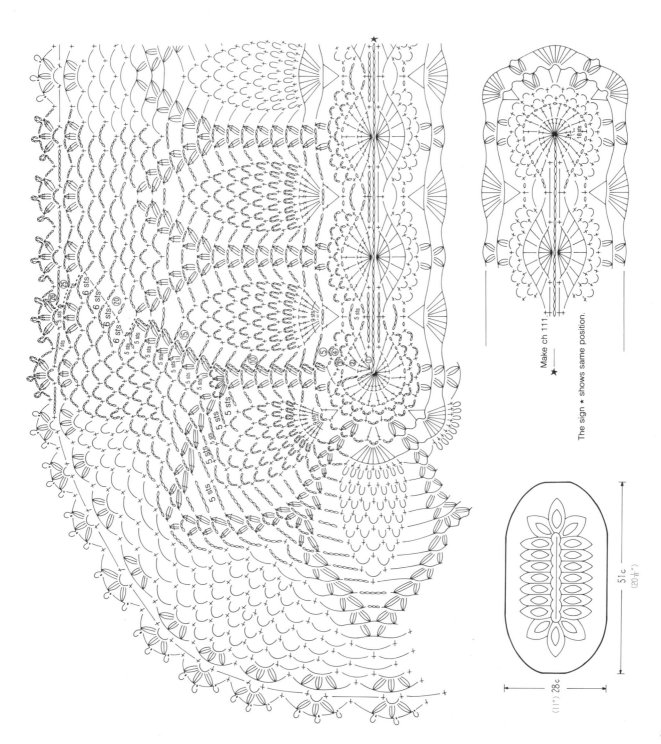

Symbols and Techniques used in this book

Chain stitch (ch) ◯

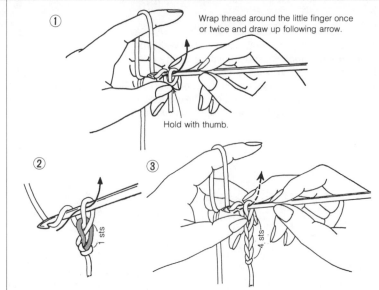

① Wrap thread around the little finger once or twice and draw up following arrow.

Hold with thumb.

② 1 sts

③ 4 sts

Two ways of making a center loop

● Making with ch

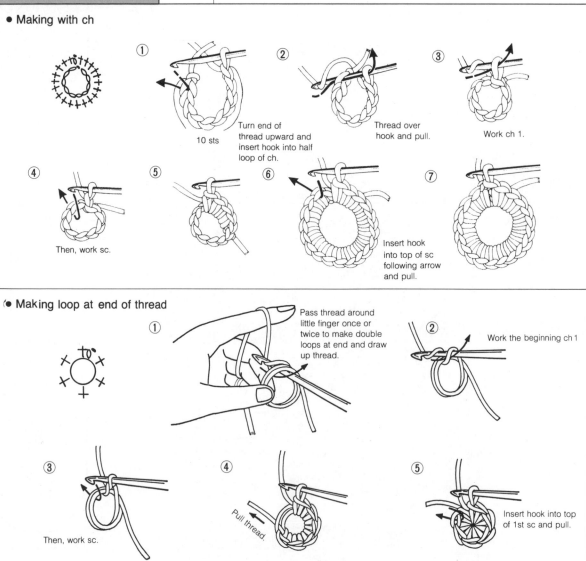

① 10 sts

Turn end of thread upward and insert hook into half loop of ch.

② Thread over hook and pull.

③ Work ch 1.

④ Then, work sc.

⑤

⑥ Insert hook into top of sc following arrow and pull.

⑦

● Making loop at end of thread

① Pass thread around little finger once or twice to make double loops at end and draw up thread.

② Work the beginning ch 1

③ Then, work sc.

④ Pull thread.

⑤ Insert hook into top of 1st sc and pull.

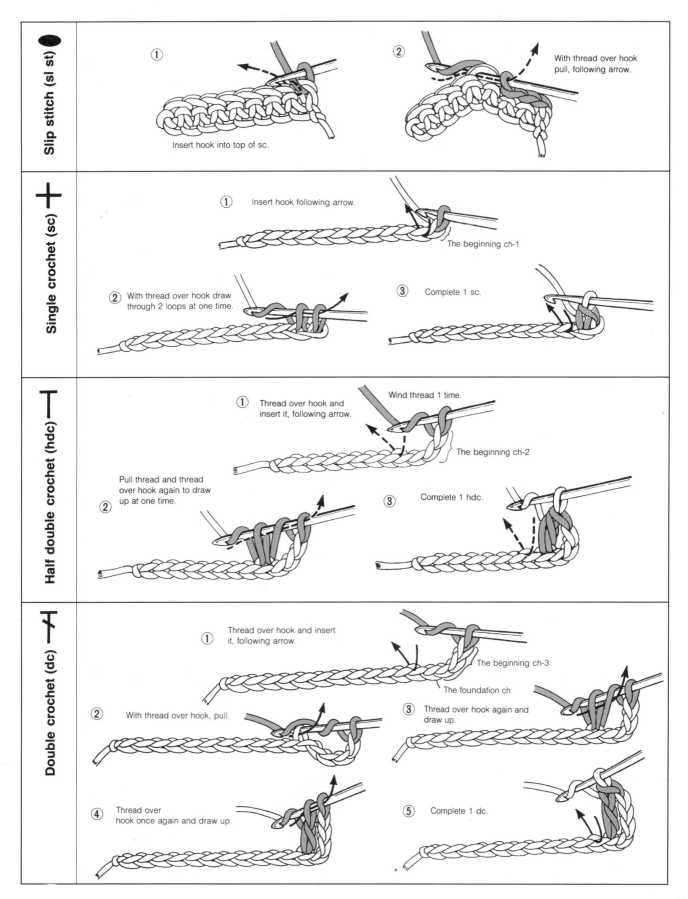

Slip stitch (sl st)

① Insert hook into top of sc.

② With thread over hook pull, following arrow.

Single crochet (sc)

① Insert hook following arrow.

The beginning ch-1

② With thread over hook draw through 2 loops at one time.

③ Complete 1 sc.

Half double crochet (hdc)

① Thread over hook and insert it, following arrow.

Wind thread 1 time.

The beginning ch-2

② Pull thread and thread over hook again to draw up at one time.

③ Complete 1 hdc.

Double crochet (dc)

① Thread over hook and insert it, following arrow.

The beginning ch-3

The foundation ch

② With thread over hook, pull.

③ Thread over hook again and draw up.

④ Thread over hook once again and draw up.

⑤ Complete 1 dc.

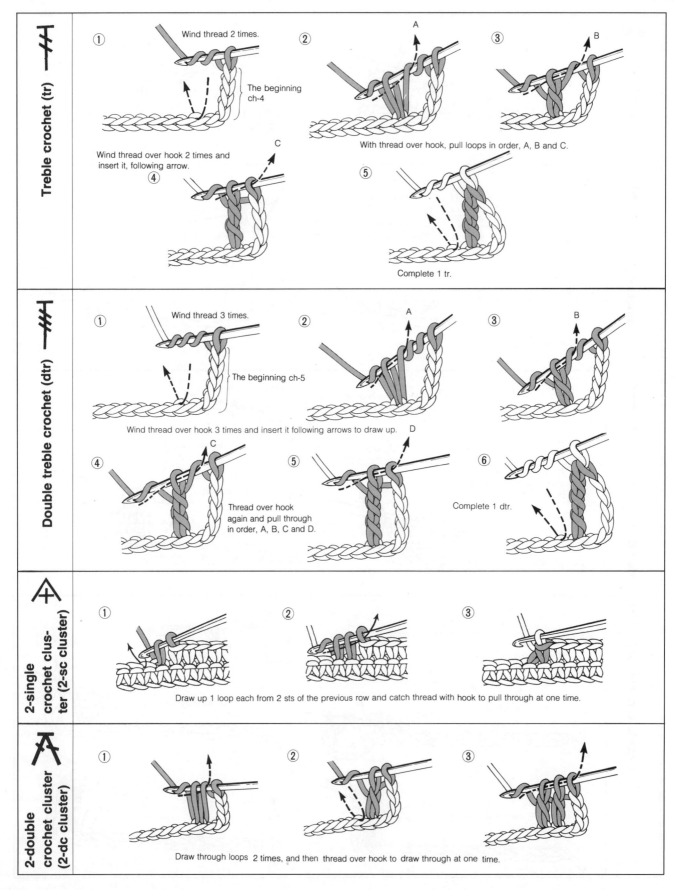

Treble crochet (tr)

① Wind thread 2 times.

The beginning ch-4

Wind thread over hook 2 times and insert it, following arrow.

② A

③ B

With thread over hook, pull loops in order, A, B and C.

④ C

⑤ Complete 1 tr.

Double treble crochet (dtr)

① Wind thread 3 times.

The beginning ch-5

Wind thread over hook 3 times and insert it following arrows to draw up.

② A

③ B

④ C

⑤ D Thread over hook again and pull through in order, A, B, C and D.

⑥ Complete 1 dtr.

2-single crochet cluster (2-sc cluster)

① ② ③

Draw up 1 loop each from 2 sts of the previous row and catch thread with hook to pull through at one time.

2-double crochet cluster (2-dc cluster)

① ② ③

Draw through loops 2 times, and then thread over hook to draw through at one time.

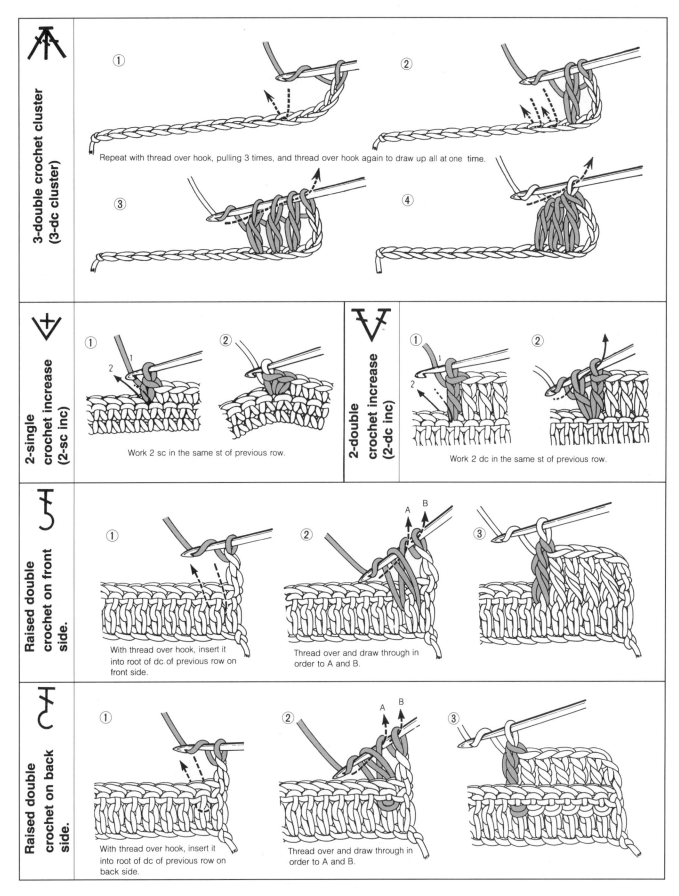

3-double crochet cluster (3-dc cluster)

① ②

Repeat with thread over hook, pulling 3 times, and thread over hook again to draw up all at one time.

③ ④

2-single crochet increase (2-sc inc)

① ②

Work 2 sc in the same st of previous row.

2-double crochet increase (2-dc inc)

① ②

Work 2 dc in the same st of previous row.

Raised double crochet on front side.

① ② A B ③

With thread over hook, insert it into root of dc of previous row on front side.

Thread over and draw through in order to A and B.

Raised double crochet on back side.

① ② A B ③

With thread over hook, insert it into root of dc of previous row on back side.

Thread over and draw through in order to A and B.

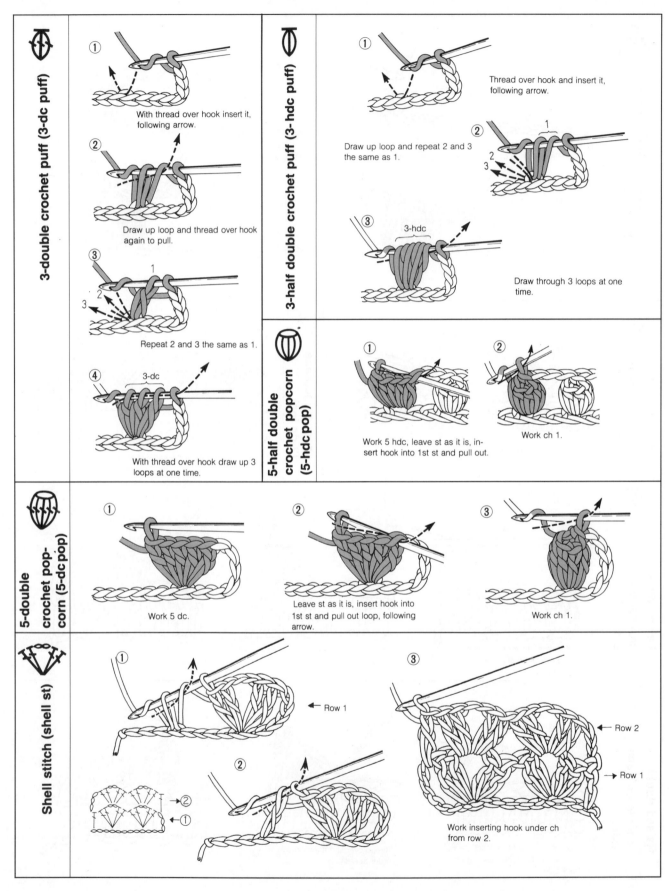

3-double crochet puff (3-dc puff)

① With thread over hook insert it, following arrow.

② Draw up loop and thread over hook again to pull.

③ Repeat 2 and 3 the same as 1.

④ 3-dc — With thread over hook draw up 3 loops at one time.

3-half double crochet puff (3-hdc puff)

① Thread over hook and insert it, following arrow.

② Draw up loop and repeat 2 and 3 the same as 1.

③ 3-hdc — Draw through 3 loops at one time.

5-half double crochet popcorn (5-hdc pop)

① Work 5 hdc, leave st as it is, insert hook into 1st st and pull out.

② Work ch 1.

5-double crochet pop-corn (5-dc pop)

① Work 5 dc.

② Leave st as it is, insert hook into 1st st and pull out loop, following arrow.

③ Work ch 1.

Shell stitch (shell st)

① ← Row 1

② →②
→①

③ ← Row 2
→ Row 1
Work inserting hook under ch from row 2.

94

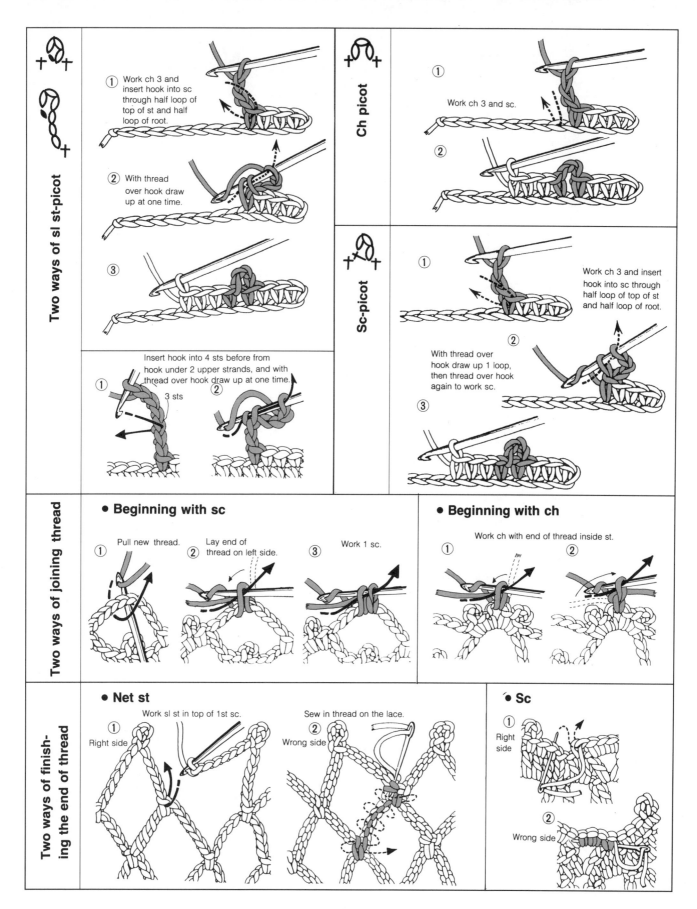

Two ways of sl st-picot

① Work ch 3 and insert hook into sc through half loop of top of st and half loop of root.

② With thread over hook draw up at one time.

③

Insert hook into 4 sts before from hook under 2 upper strands, and with thread over hook draw up at one time.

① 3 sts ②

Ch picot

① Work ch 3 and sc.

②

Sc-picot

① Work ch 3 and insert hook into sc through half loop of top of st and half loop of root.

② With thread over hook draw up 1 loop, then thread over hook again to work sc.

③

Two ways of joining thread

● **Beginning with sc**

① Pull new thread. ② Lay end of thread on left side. ③ Work 1 sc.

● **Beginning with ch**

Work ch with end of thread inside st.

① ②

Two ways of finishing the end of thread

● **Net st**

① Right side. Work sl st in top of 1st sc.

② Wrong side. Sew in thread on the lace.

● **Sc**

① Right side

② Wrong side

95

To Finish Crochet Lace Neatly

It is a matter of course to work all stitches alike and make the pattern neat and smooth, but after completing your crochet do no skip the important step of finishing because it is what makes your work excellent. Here are simple ways of finishing for beginners. Select one that suits the appearance, purpose, and feeling of your work.

Instruments for finishing

① Ironing board (soft and well padded to protect switches) ② Iron ③ Covering cloth ④ Finishing board ⑤ Transparent vinyl ⑥ Marking pin or finishing pin for handicrafts ⑦ Water sprayer ⑧ Detergent ⑨ Spray starch
Check the thread ends of the work before finishing.

If work is clean

If your work is clean and neat, iron it without washing it. The more the lace is washed the more it loses its gloss, so it is best to iron it as it is if you can.
① Place the finishing board with guidelines on the ironing board and cover it with transparent vinyl.
How to draw guidelines Fix the center and draw a circle to the finished size. Divide the radius into 3 to 5 parts and draw inner circles depending on the size of the work. Then, draw division lines according to the number of patterns made radially. If your work is made with 8 patterns around, draw 8 lines. The lines let you position the patterns; conversely, too many lines make it difficult to identify the stress on a pattern. Decide the number that are best for your work.

② Turn the work over on a board and pin it at the center first. Taking care with the design, the straight and curved lines, pin along the guidelines, pulling to position the pattern neatly. When the work is well stretched and before ironing, remove the center pin.

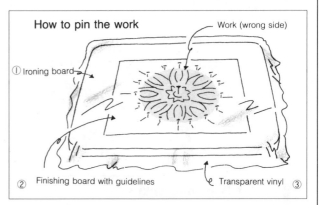

③ **For a soft finish:** Spray water over the work and adjust the warp of stitches and the shape of picot or net. At this time, adjust from the whole work to parts, parts to details and details to stitches.
For a hard finish: Apply starch over the work. Spray starch is easy to use and avoids the problems caused by lumpy starch or rusty tapwater.

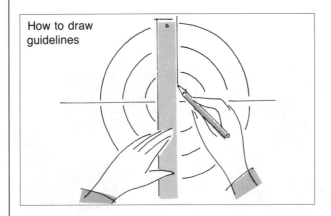

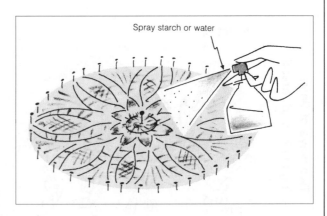

④ Apply cover cloth and press only from above with an iron set at high temperature to fix stitches. Be careful not to burn the work. Do not move the iron or the stitches will be unkempt and the pins useless. Remove the pins after the work is completely dry. Be careful not to touch vinyl with the iron.

The sizes of doilies and centerpieces given in each patterns are measurements after finishing. Therefore, the crocheted size is smaller than the finished size.

cotton it shrinks after washing. Also, stitches and the whole work are wavy, so fix the center, pull the work outward rather tightly, then pin it.

④ Dry it in a shady and airy place, and when it is 80-percent dry remove the center pin. Apply cover cloth and iron. Press only from above with the iron and be careful not to move it. Remove pins after the work is completely dry.

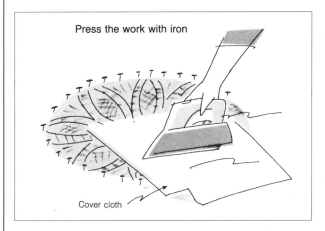

Press the work with iron

Cover cloth

How to wash

Shake or squeeze

If your work is not flat

If your work has uneven stitches and a frill or a turned up rim and is not flag, finish it in the same way as neat work. The frill becomes uneven when the length of one stitch is not enough for the width of the stitch. Finish stretching the length of that work. The rim of a work turns up when the length of a stitch is too much for its width. Finish stretching the width of that work.

B. When there are spots on the work

Remove spots as soon as you find them

① If it is a small spot, place the work on a towel and tap it with a cloth soaked in a soap solution. Spots will be removed by changing the position of the towel and tapping repeatedly.

② Light spots will be removed by washing. If spots cannot be removed easily, soak the work in solution of 1 liter water and 10 g detergent or boil the piece for 10 minutes to 1 hour, depending on the spots.

③ The rest of the procedure is the same as ③ to ④.

If the work is not clean

Since the beauty of lace is in its fresh, crisp appearance, stains or spots ruin all your good work. Wash soiled lace immediately.

A. If the work is soiled

① Dissolve detergent in tepid water and wash the work, shaking or squeezing softly. Rinse repeatedly until the water becomes clear, then wrap it in a towel to dry.

② Crochet cotton contains little starch, so apply some after washing.

③ Put a finishing board on the ironing board, place vinyl on it and turn the work over on it, then pin it. Since the crochet thread is

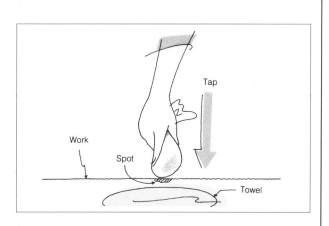

Tap

Work

Spot

Towel

How to make beautiful frills

① Fix the work on the ironing board in the same manner as lace without frills. At this time, part of the frills are tightly stretched lengthwise.

② Apply thicker starch on the frills than the center parts. Spray starch in 2 or 3 sections, since spraying all at once takes too much time to dry.

③ When it is 80-percent dry, apply cover cloth and iron lengthwise, then remove the pins.

④ Decide the number and position of frills according to the pattern, but remember the number of frills increase when the frills are small. Place the work face up and put the thumb and fore-finger of the left hand on the inside part of a frill. Hold and stretch the fabric upward and outward with the right hand, adjusting the shape with your thumb. Be careful not to press frills already made. After completing all the frills, adjust outer lace with fingers.

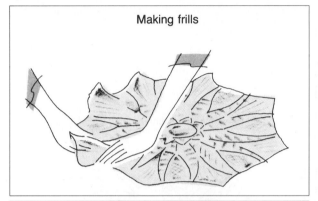

Making frills

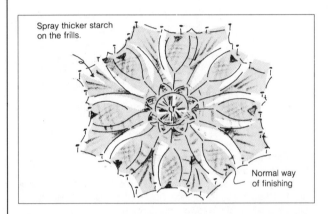

Spray thicker starch on the frills.

Normal way of finishing

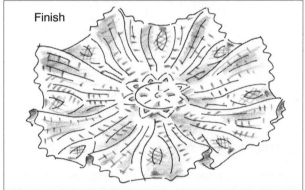

Finish

PINEAPPLE PATTERN

The pineapple pattern is said to have originated with the pinecone design found on the textiles and china of India and Persia. Since the shape of the pinecone looks like a pineapple, it became known as the pineapple pattern. But it is the most popular pattern with lovers of crochet because it is gorgeous looking. The basic pattern, shown in the chart at right, is worked with a net stitch on the base shaped fan with double crochet (or treble crochet) and decreased 1 loop on each row until the last loop. The size of pineapple depends on whether double crochet or treble crochet is used on the base. Though the shell stitch, popcorn, puff and double crochet are all worked around a pineapple pattern, the shell stitch is used most often.

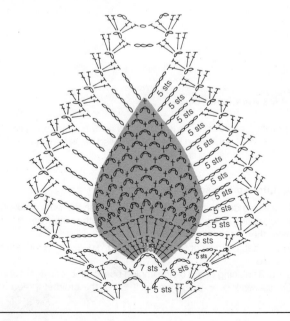